From Research to the Music Classroom

Applications of Research in Music Technology

William L. Berz and Judith Bowman

MENC
MUSIC EDUCATORS NATIONAL CONFERENCE

Music Educators National Conference
1806 Robert Fulton Drive
Reston, VA 22091-4348

Printed in the United States of America
ISBN 1-56545-026-4

Contents

Foreword v

Chapter 1. Introduction 1
Need for technology research 2
Identification of research/development cycles 3
Models of instruction: Application and CAI software 6
Models of instruction: Media orientation 11

Chapter 2. The Role of Music Technology in Schools 15
Basic musicianship 15
Performance skills 22
Creativity 26
Curriculum design 28
Testing 31
Role of the computer and electronic instruments 34
Other applications 35
Summary 36

Chapter 3. Developing New Instructional Models in CAI 39
Hypertext and hypermedia 39
Artificial intelligence 45
Robotics 51
Virtual reality 52

Chapter 4. Conclusions and Summary 55
Integrating technology into music teaching 56
Instructional choice: Special concerns 56
Transfer 56
Student developmental levels 57
Learning strategies 57
Expertise 58
Procedures 58
Student response 58
Implementation time 59
Emerging technologies 59
Technological tips 59
Summary 61

References 63

Glossary 87

Foreword

More than twenty years have lapsed since the publication of the first monographs in the MENC series *From Research to the Music Classroom*. In the foreword to that original series, it was noted that "research, even with all of its frailties, is the best way mankind has yet devised for unearthing objective truth." In the intervening twenty years, research in all fields of human endeavor has expanded enormously. While it may be debatable as to whether humankind is now any closer to unearthing "objective truth," it is indisputable that in the past twenty years we have witnessed an unparalleled knowledge explosion. It is that knowledge explosion, especially in the area of music teaching and learning, that makes the publication of this new *From Research to the Music Classroom* series so important.

The purpose of each book in this series is threefold:

- to identify specific topics of interest to music teachers at all levels
- to summarize and synthesize all the research that has been done related to the specific topic
- to draw some tentative conclusions based on the research and make some practical suggestions for music teachers.

Research findings can be an invaluable resource for music teachers at all levels. One word of caution is necessary, however. Research is a continuing process and as new evidence emerges and old evidence is reinterpreted, beliefs and conclusions must be adjusted accordingly. Research findings are rarely applicable in all teaching situations, and sound judgment must be used in interpreting those findings. Research, however, can provide direction for music teachers interested in evaluating and updating their teaching on a regular basis. It is that ideal to which this series is dedicated.

—Charles A. Elliott
Series Editor
From Research to the Music Classroom

Chapter 1

Introduction

> In recent years it has become fashionable to talk about two industrial revolutions. The first, which unfolded during the nineteenth century, was based on the heavy, capital-intensive industries–coal, iron, steel, petroleum, railroads, steam engines, electricity, and automobiles–which transformed a rural, agricultural America into an urban, industrial nation. Many observers believe that the second industrial revolution, driven by the electronic data-processing technology of the last half of the twentieth century, will prove to be just as important and cataclysmic as the first. In less than forty-five years, electronic computers have evolved from large, one-of-a-kind dinosaurs with only limited utility outside the laboratory into compact personal computers with applications in the office, the factory, and the home. During this period the number of computers in the United States has risen dramatically from one in 1946 to an estimated 240 in 1955, to 165,000 in 1975, to uncountable millions today. (Nash, 1989, p. 7)

Practical implementation of technology in schools has, unfortunately, not proceeded as rapidly as many observers expected. The most obvious problem has been limited school funding–computers and other technological devices, such as piano labs and synthesizers, are expensive. In many cases, schools have been limited in adopting technology-based instruction simply because they are unable to purchase the equipment. In many situations, schools have purchased one or two computers for each classroom; this limits use since only a few students can use the equipment at any given time. Music teachers may be even more limited than classroom teachers in this regard.

Research cited in the popular press (Krondracke, 1992) quotes government figures from the 1991-92 school year showing numbers of computers per student. Even in the states with the highest ratios, the level has not reached 10 students per computer; the worst states have ratios of about 30 students per computer. Other statistics quoted indicate that only about 39% of American high school students use computers at school (Krondracke, 1992). Also alarming but not surprising, economically disadvantaged students have much less chance of using computers at school than do students who attend affluent schools.

These figures do not reflect that many schools own only old and outdated machines. Few in the business or research world would consider use of the "Model-T" of educational computers: the Apple IIe. In some classrooms the only computers that are found are outmoded machines, cast off from other sources. From a survey of music educators in Michigan, Dunnigan (1993) found that the Apple II generation of computers was the overwhelming computer-of-choice for most teachers. Although these machines are still very usable (Apfelstadt, 1992), they are not capable of most of the modern applications, and most software designers are no longer writing for that platform. Many schools do not have money to purchase software or to repair broken computers, with the result that machines sit idle.

Yet maybe an even larger problem faced in introducing technology into the classroom is the lack of appropriate instructional models and practical teaching methods. The technology is so new and continues to evolve so rapidly that instructional theory is not always clearly defined. Many teachers and school systems do not hold a clear image of how computerized technology should be used for best advantage. A survey of instrumental music educators in Michigan revealed that administrative tasks account for the vast majority of all music-related activities performed on the computer (Dunnigan, 1993); this would not seem to be the best use of technology. The promise has been great, but practical implementation has not met most expectations.

Also, many teachers do not know how to operate the equipment, let alone use it effectively in the classroom. Teacher retraining has not taken place to any great degree and many institutions of higher learning, for a variety of reasons, have not been committed to training new teachers in educational computing and instructional technology.

Need for technology research

Often computer use in education has been championed based on intuition and informal observation. This is probably somewhat justified and understandable given the contemporary nature and uniqueness of the field. However, there is need to examine instructional practices in more systematic ways to see which approaches are the most valuable. Some research has been conducted to justify computer use based on more tangible criteria:

cost effectiveness (Niemiec, Sikorski, & Walberg, 1989), instructional effectiveness (Kulik & Kulik, 1987), instructional and research suitability (Kozma, 1991), and positive student attitudes (Kulik & Kulik, 1987).

Meta-analyses have been performed on hundreds of studies of computer-assisted instruction (CAI) in all subject areas at elementary, secondary, and college levels (the instruction is also called computer-based instruction or CBI). The meta-analyses reveal statistically significant differences in achievement at each level in favor of students who used CAI (Kulik, Bangert-Downs, & Williams, 1983; Kulik, Kulik, & Bangert-Downs, 1984; Kulik, Kulik, & Cohen, 1980; Kulik & Kulik, 1987). Meta-analysis has also been done on interactive video, supporting its effectiveness as an instructional approach with identification of an effect similar to that of computer-assisted instruction (McNeil & Nelson, 1991). Hofstetter (1985) stated that "achievement effect sizes are greater in more recent studies than in earlier ones. It is encouraging to note that as computer-based instruction grows older, it is getting better. Moreover, those studies that recorded learning times showed that not only does CBI produce higher achievement scores, but it also significantly reduces the time needed for instruction" (p. 2).

There is considerable debate among researchers as to the validity of studies that compare traditional and technologically centered instruction (Clark, 1983, 1985; Kulik, Kulik, & Bangert-Drowns, 1985; Kozma, 1991). It is important to investigate how best to utilize this technology for educational gain. This question might be a more important and valid question to address rather than that of comparing the effectiveness of traditional versus technological methodology in order to justify its existence.

Identification of research/development cycles

Research and development of specific computer applications has followed definite cycles: development of a specific technology, usually unrelated to any educational goal, adaptation of the technology for educational use, conducting feasibility studies to determine development and implementation, and conducting effectiveness studies. A new cycle begins as instructional flaws are identified through research and practice, and as new technologies are developed. Figure 1 summarizes this pattern.

This pattern is really quite logical. First, a specific technology must be developed. Second, it must be adapted to fit a purpose—in this case, some educational goal. Practical development of a specific application comes next. Following this, the technology must be evaluated to see if it actually accomplishes the stated

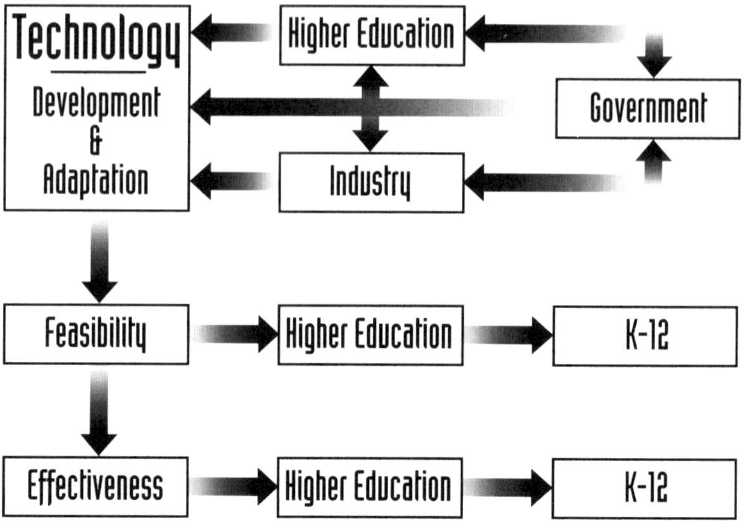

Figure 1. Evolutionary cycle of technology research

goal. With the start of each cycle, new research strategies appear and new instructional theories are developed that are better suited for the new technology.

Four distinct research cycles related to educational computing have been identified–each cycle linked to specific technological developments. Although the specific dates are somewhat arbitrary, the periods are (1) Early Period (to 1965), (2) Mainframe Period (1965-1978), (3) Microcomputer/Traditional CAI Period (1978-1989), and (4) Emerging Technologies Period (1989-). The identification of these research cycles is important since it places current research in a defining framework and illustrates why research and teaching models have changed so profoundly every ten years.

The first period, the early era of CAI, began with the development of the computer and lasted until approximately 1965. The first computers were not developed for educational use, but were developed for use in plotting missile trajectories (Alessi & Trollip, 1985; Nash, 1989). The earliest uses of CAI, dating from the late 1950s, were by members of the computer industry who developed programs to train their own personnel (Suppes & Macken, 1978). The development of high-level authoring languages opened computer usage for educational institutions (Hofstetter, 1981b) and led to the first true efforts in institutional CAI. Governmental agencies, private industry, and higher education often joined forces–formally or informally–in the development of new technologies.

The second period was typified by mainframe applications and lasted from approximately 1965 until 1978. Beginning in the early and middle 1960s, significant work was completed at several universities, illustrating that CAI had potential for use in education (Hofstetter, 1981b). Some of the most notable work was performed at the University of Illinois with the development of the PLATO system. Other important early research was completed at Stanford University, Florida State University, University of Texas, and Brigham Young University (Suppes & Macken, 1978). This period also saw rather significant federal funding to develop technological applications (Hofstetter, 1981b).

The earliest research in music education was dominated by feasibility studies, which describe the development and/or implementation of specific applications, often for use at a university (Allvin, 1970; Deihl, 1971; Deihl & Radocy, 1969; Hofstetter, 1975; Kuhn, 1974; Kuhn & Allvin, 1967; Peters, 1974; Placek, 1972, 1974). Later research was dominated by effectiveness studies (Arenson, 1979; Hofstetter, 1978, 1979, 1980, 1981a, 1981c; Hullfish, 1972; Von Feldt, 1971). These studies generally either compared a new technological approach with traditional approaches or evaluated it in light of some outside criterion such as time efficiency or achievement scores. This era of research has been well detailed by Eddins (1981), McGreer (1984), Peters (1981, 1992), and Robinson (1987).

The release of the Apple II microcomputer in 1978 had enormous impact on educational computing and was the defining event of the third research/development period. The Apple II computer was widely released into K-12 schools, and most early courseware was designed for it (Alessi & Trollip, 1991). The Apple computer was followed by the introduction of the IBM-PC in 1981 and the Macintosh computer in 1984. The introduction of these relatively inexpensive machines allowed practical implementation of computer technology in the K-12 classroom and altered previous instructional models. Dunnigan (1993) states that computers can be found in almost every elementary and secondary school nationwide, whereas only a decade ago computers were relatively rare. This is due to the increasing availability, affordability, and portability of personal computers.

Many studies in the late 1970s and early 1980s detailed the development and practical implementation of microcomputer-based educational applications in music (Hultberg, Hultberg, & Tenny, 1979; Peters, 1979; Wilson, 1981). Effectiveness studies (Deal, 1985; Hesser, 1988; Malave, 1990/1991; Sanders, 1980; Weeks, 1987) followed. Much of this research was influenced by earlier work with mainframe computers.

Beginning in the late 1980s, a new research trend started to emerge. Two primary factors caused the research cycle of development-feasibility-effectiveness to begin yet again. The first factor related to the improvements in hardware (power and speed) and the ability to link the computer with other devices such as the compact disc, the videodisc, and MIDI equipment. The second factor was the formulation of new instructional models that do not follow the theoretical underpinnings of the older CAI software. Some earlier CAI programs had been criticized because of their behavioral character. The newer instructional models—hypermedia, artificial intelligence, and virtual reality—have been, at least in theory, more instructionally flexible. An arbitrary starting date for the fourth research/development period has been set as 1989, based on publication of the first commercial hypermedia application in music, "Beethoven Symphony No. 9" by Winter. The term virtual reality was also introduced in 1989. Since the late 1980s, there have been a number of feasibility studies, particularly in the area of hypermedia. To this point, there have been very few effectiveness studies.

Models of instruction: Application and CAI software

Actual computer use is defined by the equipment's designed purpose. With computers, this definition is determined largely by the design of the software. In education these designs are application and CAI software.

Teacher Tip

Most technology has a very narrowly defined purpose. Make sure that your instructional goals are realistic within the limitations of the particular technology.

Application (tool) software is designed to make some function easier to perform. The most common types of general application software include word processors, data bases, and spreadsheets; each lets the user execute some function more easily than would be possible without it. These kinds of application programs have been used with great success in completing the many administrative tasks associated with music education.

Also, many examples of application programs are content-specific to music: notation programs, sequencers and other sound manipulation tools, composition software, and software for writing marching band drills. These programs hold enormous potential in the areas of music performance, composition, and education.

Teacher Tip

Sequencers are very effective tools for teaching composition since they allow easy manipulation of sound. Students can hear and then revise their compositions.

Although application programs can be used with great success in the classroom, their design is not intended for teaching; they were created to ease the performance of some concrete task. When this software is used in the classroom, the teacher must provide the instructional structure, employing the program as a highly specific tool. For example, sequencers provide a platform for relatively easy manipulation of sound—a task that was not easily accomplished before the development of this software. Obviously, this would be extremely valuable in teaching composition. By themselves, however, sequencers do not provide a direct educational gain. Students may learn significantly from using them, but the instructional organization is not inherently present in the software. Either the learning is strictly discovery based, or the student must receive guidance from the teacher on the music fundamentals to be gleaned by using the software.

Teacher Tip

Teachers must provide the lesson structure when using computerized application programs. Application software does not teach, but teachers can use it to teach.

In contrast, CAI's primary purpose is to teach, and therefore it is designed specifically to meet this function. CAI is not necessarily superior to application software for the classroom, but it is different. Its scope is usually quite narrow and defined–the teaching of some specific instructional outcome–as opposed to the less limited, but less defined nature of application software.

As in other forms of teaching, CAI must follow some instructional model. Alessi and Trollip (1991) present a four-step instructional model that is suited for this approach: presenting information, guiding the student, student practice, and assessing student learning. Their model was formulated from an examination of research of classroom instruction.

Most traditional CAI is rooted in one or more of the steps of this model. By using this model and examining available CAI applications, Alessi and Trollip (1991) defined five major types of computer-based instruction: tutorials, drills, simulations, games, and tests. Many current programs incorporate more than one type in an application, for example, tutorials and drills.

CAI: Tutorials

Ideally, tutorials are aimed at satisfying the first two components of the instructional model: presenting information and guiding the student. They usually do not engage the students in extended practice nor do they assess learning. Many tutorials only perform the first function: presenting information. This emphasis on presentation is still the case in many new applications. For example, most of the audio-CD tutorials developed beginning in 1989 (Voyager and Warner publications) give little student guidance and may actually provide less guidance than did the older CAI programs of the mid-1980s.

Teacher Tip

Tutorial software can be used for supplementary instruction on specific problem areas.

In tutorials, the computer is the presenter of information–a teacher substitute of sorts. Subject matter may be quite narrow or very broad depending on the specific program. Different programs allow the learner varying degrees of control. In many of the early tutorials, the presentation of information was determined solely by the computer. The current audio-CD tutorials allow the student almost total control in terms of content, sequence, and mode of presentation (text, verbal presentation, music, animation, or pictures). This contrasts sharply with traditional classroom models where the teacher largely controls presentation.

Alessi and Trollip (1991) assert that tutorials should also guide the student through the information. In the guidance mode, the student must respond to computer queries, with the computer providing feedback and adapting the instruction. Most early CAI tutorials do not do this, possibly because of computer limitations. The lack of student guidance in computer tutorials has been a consistent criticism and is one reason for the increased attention given to artificial intelligence, where the computer can adapt presentation based upon student interaction with the machine.

CAI: Drill and practice

Drill-and-practice software satisfies the third component of the instructional model, namely drill. This kind of software is probably the most commonly found type of CAI. Drills are not intended to provide new information; they provide practice material under the assumption that the student is already familiar with the material to at least some degree.

This kind of CAI probably has received significant criticism from educators. Some state that drills can be boring (McArthur, 1992). "Many educators claim drills do not capitalize upon the power of the computer and that drills can as easily be accomplished through workbooks or flashcards" (Alessi & Trollip, 1991, p. 91). Others criticize drills as being overly behavioristic.

On the whole, these criticisms are unfair. Many cognitive psychologists recognize the need for practice as a vital part of encoding information into long-term memory—a necessary part of effective learning. The research literature on this subject is rich (Baddeley, 1990). Computers can easily outperform flashcard or workbook approaches for several reasons. First, computers can provide almost unlimited practice exercises; workbook examples are limited. Second, computers do not tire; teachers using flashcards do tire or face time limitations. Third, practice sessions can be customized to fit the practice requirements of each student; teachers can do this only if working with one student at a time, which is not always practical or possible. Fourth, if students are working alone on the computer, they do not face the pressures of criticism from teachers or peers. Students may have less fear of answering incorrectly when removed from the pressures of maintaining self-esteem in the normal classroom setting, and therefore they may take a more active role in the practice session.

Actually, drill-and-practice software might be one of the most valuable types of CAI now available. It is best used in those areas that require extended repeated practice, such as in hearing intervals in ear training. The computer can provide the student with unlimited practice in a nonthreatening, self-paced environment. The fact that the model is not the most up-to-date type of application should not inhibit its use.

Some drill-and-practice software has been justifiably criticized in that some programs do not provide meaningful feedback. This causes students to practice and reinforce mistakes.

> **Teacher Tip**
>
> ***Use drill-and-practice software for reinforcing basic skills such as note naming and ear training. Do not expect drill-and-practice software to teach concepts.***

Many people expect drill-and-practice software to teach concepts. This is not the case and is the root of much of the criticism of these programs. Drills provide only a limited segment of the instructional process–student practice. These programs can serve a very valuable function when used appropriately.

CAI: Simulations

In simulations, students learn by performing activities in a context similar to a real world setting. Very often the real-life setting may be dangerous, as in the case of flight simulators, or may be impossible to reproduce in the real world, as in the case of duplicating a historical time period. It is an experiential approach that allows students to learn by doing.

In theory, simulations could encompass any or all of the four components of the instructional model. Alessi and Trollip (1991) classify simulations into two subcategories: those that teach *about* something and those that teach *how to* do something. *About* simulations deal with some process or some physical property. An example might be a simulation program that lets the student become the political leader of a state where he or she must cope with some specific dilemma. The computer presents a series of planned and random events to which the student must react. This software forces students to develop problem-solving strategies within some specific context. *How to* simulations place the student in some position in order to develop a skill; flight simulators are examples. While a number of simulations have been written in educational contexts, little work of this type has been done in music education. Simulations have become quite popular as arcade games.

Virtual reality represents the evolution of simulation software. Virtual reality attempts to place the user in an actual environment. Ideally, the user should feel that he or she is interacting with the real world and not with a computer. Although the potential for educational gain is great, technological barriers limit actual use at this time.

CAI: Instructional games

Instructional games are modifications of basic types of CAI, most notably drill and practice or simulation, with the addition of a game component. Ideally, games provide greater motivation for students than the usual CAI; therefore, students should gain more from the experience. Unfortunately, many instructional games do not have a clear educational orientation; the educational component of the game may be so veiled that no learning takes place. Other games, when compared to the arcade variety, pale to such an extent that they fail to motivate students. For an instructional game to be successful, it must both teach and motivate.

Teacher Tip

When using an instructional game, make sure that it is truly instructional and not an empty activity.

CAI: Testing

The use of computers in testing may take many different forms. First, many traditional CAI programs include a quiz where records are maintained by the computer for use by the teacher. Not only are students able to test their learning and receive appropriate feedback, but in many cases, teachers are able to see progress since the computer can easily maintain student records.

There are other ways to incorporate computers in assessment: using the computer as an aid in constructing tests and using the computer to administer tests (see Alessi & Trollip, 1991, p. 205). These approaches are well established; most teachers are very familiar with computer-scored tests. These approaches can save considerable time in developing and scoring tests.

There are many new approaches for using computers in assessment. One of the most exciting developments is by Peters (1992), who details the development of techniques that allow the computer to assess accuracy in singing in a specified context. Adaptive testing is also an important development in computerized assessment in music; the machine presents items of differing difficulty, based on the student's response to previous questions. By using sophisticated programming and new statistical models, these new computer-administered adaptive tests can save enormous time while retaining high levels of validity and reliability (Vispoel & Coffman, 1992).

Also, computers can be employed as research tools, used to record student behaviors, as well as to collect and analyze data (Bowers & Tsai, 1990). This approach can be utilized for a variety of purposes, ranging from studies of human/machine interaction to general assessment devices.

Models of instruction: Media orientation

Much of the theoretical writing about technology in education focuses on the computer. However, there is also considerable interest in other technologies. Much of this research is classified under the broad category of instructional media:

> Media can be defined by its technology, symbol systems, and processing capabilities. The most obvious characteristic of a medium is its technology: the mechanical and electronic aspects that determine its function and, to some extent, its shape and other physical features. These are the characteristics that are commonly used to classify a medium such as a television, a radio, and so on. (Kozma, 1991, p. 180)

Kozma (1991) lists media forms currently found in education: books (text and pictures), television, computers, and multimedia such as interactive video, various videodisc environments, and hypermedia. The last three forms would relate to this discussion of instructional media. Of course, there are other media that are not quite as current but are still commonly found in the schools: movies, film strips, and sound recordings in various formats. All of these forms can be classified under one of Kozma's types.

Television

The popularity of such shows as "Sesame Street" has created significant interest in educational television. One of the most popularly held views is that children are highly motivated and therefore watch programs attentively and learn significantly. Research shows that when alternate activities are present, children look away from and back at the television up to 200 times per hour (Anderson & Field, 1983). Although attention varies with age, distraction periods as long as a minute are not rare (Kozma, 1991). If children do not attend to the material, of course, they will not learn.

The pace of presentation is a major factor for consideration when evaluating television as an instructional medium. The rapid pace of commercials, with as many as a dozen different scenes in a thirty-second commercial, is intended presumably to increase attention; "Sesame Street" also employs very short segments. Unfortunately, little research has been done on the effects of pace on comprehension (Kozma, 1991). Wright et al. (1984) used 16 15-minute children's television programs that varied in pace and continuity to measure comprehension. They found that the children who viewed slow-paced, high-continuity programs performed better.

Pace is a vital consideration in terms of comprehension and

memory. In television, pace is controlled totally by the producers of the program. Students are unable to slow the pace, repeat segments, or stop the program when viewing broadcast television. Students may miss an important point, and this might inhibit learning during later parts of the program. There may be too much information presented, overloading working memory. People who lack expertise in a given field would need a slower pace than would experts; content experts might become bored if the pace is too slow.

Also, research has been conducted on the relationship between audio and visual elements and the role that each plays in learning. The visual component of a presentation is particularly important, while the auditory systems carry information that helps the interpretation of the visual (Kozma, 1991).

Television certainly has had an impact on the field of music in general; for example, MTV has had enormous cultural impact. Unfortunately, the impact of educational television on music has been less dramatic. Certainly, considerably more research needs to be performed in these areas.

Multimedia and hypermedia

The areas of computers, multimedia, and hypermedia have become linked because of technological developments. The computer can control a variety of media; the processor can be a standalone unit or can be self-contained in an external device.

Multimedia is hardly a new concept and is really a very simple idea: the mixing of different media in a single presentation. Music teachers have always done this by combining music with verbal and written instructions. An old method was to use film strips or slides linked to records or tapes (Kozma, 1991); this approach was the norm for instructional media in the 1950s, 60s, and 70s.

With the advent of current computer technologies, multimedia models have changed considerably. Computers are able to manipulate and present diverse information, such as text, music, video, and graphics, and are able to control external devices such as CD players, videodisc players, and MIDI devices. The presentation can be much more complex than that which was possible just a few years ago.

Even though this kind of presentation holds great potential benefit for teaching, multimedia does have some distinct limitations that must be considered. First, users have little control over the order or pace of presentation. Multimedia is very linear; the presentation of information is determined solely by the author, much in the same way as it is with textbooks. Students are unable to seek supplemental help on those concepts that are not understood. There is little chance for students to review, limiting the ability to reinforce learning.

The structure of multimedia is not inherently educational; multimedia is simply an approach to presenting information. It may be a very effective way in which to teach, but it is up to the teacher to provide the educational framework. Otherwise it is all glitz and no substance.

Hypermedia is a specific type of multimedia that is a specialized approach to information management. There are a number of commercially developed hypermedia tutorials in music education that link the computer to an audio compact disc. This approach will be discussed in detail later in this publication.

> **Teacher Tip**
>
> ***Multimedia is a tool for teaching, but teachers must provide an instructional framework for learning to take place.***

Piano labs and synthesizers

With increasing frequency, manufacturers are developing keyboard labs and software-based lessons. Baldwin/Wurlitzer, Roland, and Yamaha have developed such systems. These labs and related materials represent an effort to integrate music technology into the traditional music education curriculum. Created on the foreign language model, these labs constitute another tool for music educators. The curricular materials focus on traditional music skills and concepts, with high technology instruments supporting one or more of many different kinds of experiences in the music teaching and learning environment.

Yamaha Corporation has carried out systematic research on its Music in Education system, and claims significant increases in both short-term and long-term achievement as measured by standardized achievement tests (Moore, 1991). Students who learned with Music in Education significantly outperformed control classes in pitch discrimination, interval discrimination, and major/minor mode discrimination. Over a period of two years, experimental groups showed more than three times the improvement of control groups in percentile rankings. The research suggests that the varied activities (singing, movement, and keyboard tasks) used in the Music in Education system resulted in greater retention than did the control approaches. It also points out increases in student interest and motivation, as well as transfer of gains in cooperative learning and creative thinking to other academic areas.

> **Teacher Tip**
>
> ***Bridge the gap between "real" music and "school" music by integrating electronic keyboards into the traditional music curriculum.***

While little or no research has been conducted using popular technologies such as Magic Piano and The Miracle Piano Teaching System, these should also be studied and assessed by music educators.

Some music teachers attest informally to the motivational value of keyboard labs, particularly for students who are at an age at which their interest in general music has begun to wane as well as for students who are not participating in performance classes. Electronic keyboards in these situations are used to promote both music literacy and musical creativity. Other teachers observe that integration of high technology into the traditional music curriculum also appears to increase public perception of the relevance of the music education program. Many believe that music educators must continue to integrate technology into traditional curricula to keep pace with the other subject areas that are following this direction (Appell, 1993; Chamberlin, Clark, & Svengalis, 1993; Wiggins, 1993).

Teacher Tip

Integrate MIDI concepts into traditional piano classes using new keyboard lab systems.

Synthesizers are finding increasing use in music classrooms, both linked to computers and as stand-alone instruments. Synthesizers are being used as substitutes for acoustic instruments in traditional performance ensembles, as well as being used in new synthesizer ensembles. They are being employed with some frequency in music theory classes.

There is little research detailing how synthesizers are actually used in the schools. There are many questions that need to be addressed. For example, what are the effects of using synthesizers as substitutes for acoustic instruments (e.g., tuba) in traditional performance ensembles? Are these technologies being used to teach composition in K–12 education? What is the effect of visual display on composition since graphic representation is used normally instead of musical notation in these devices?

Teacher Tip

Think of synthesizers not as machines but as ***musical instruments*** *with their own unique performance techniques and requirements.*

Miscellaneous devices

For quite some time, teachers have employed special electronic devices to help teach certain concepts. The most notable example is the electronic intonation tuner, which is employed to provide a visual cue to assist in achieving correct intonation. These devices have been used with great success in instrumental music. More recently, special devices have been developed that are dedicated machines for assisting in the teaching of certain concepts. The TAP Master and Pitch Master of Temporal Acuity Products have received wide-scale use for teaching ear training.

There are other techniques and devices that will be used with increasing frequency as teaching tools. These include voice processors, specialized recording devices (e.g., direct-to-disk recording), and digital sound editors.

Chapter 2

The Role of Music Technology in Schools

Basic musicianship

The largest body of research in computer-assisted instruction has been directed toward basic musicianship skills: music reading, sight-singing, and pitch discrimination studies have been conducted across the entire spectrum from pre-elementary through college. Ear training studies that emphasize interval and chord identification and melodic, harmonic, and rhythmic dictation have been concentrated at the college level, while elementary through secondary ear training has emphasized pitch discrimination, tonal memory, and simpler ear training tasks. Studies of skill development in error detection have been concentrated at the college level, particularly in music teacher education courses. Music listening experiments are being carried out at the secondary and college levels in connection with development of computer environments.

Music reading and pitch discrimination

Higher education. CAI was found as effective as traditional instruction in the areas of note names, key signatures, and rhythm examples for college-level elementary education majors who substituted a 50-minute CAI drill-and-practice session on fundamentals of notation and rhythm for one traditional class per week (totaling 9 classes). In the areas of note types and counting, traditional instruction was found more effective (Jacobsen, 1986/1987).

Secondary. Secondary school students (Grades 9-12) in beginning keyboard classes who used basal instruction, supplemented by CAI designed to improve vertical/horizontal reading skills, showed higher achievement on a performance test than did a control group, although posttests revealed no significant differences in achievement (M. Holland, 1987).

Commercial CAI software can be an effective adjunct to regular classroom music instruction at the junior high level. King (1988/1989) reported the following effects of computer-assisted instruction on the achievement of seventh-grade students: Seventh-grade students who used commercial CAI programs to study fundamentals of music theory as a supplement to traditional instruction in general music, band, and orchestra classes showed higher levels of achievement than did control groups in each area. Areas of greater achievement included note identification, clef identification, major-minor discrimination, pitch discrimination, and rhythm discrimination. Students in a half-period CAI band/orchestra group showed a higher level of achievement in note and clef identification and in major-minor discrimination. A general-music CAI group scored higher in pitch discrimination, rhythm discrimination, notes and clefs, incomplete measures, and the total. A whole-period CAI group scored higher on rhythm discrimination, notes and clefs, and the total. Students who had prior instrumental instruction realized the greater benefits. Most of the seventh-grade CAI users had positive attitudes toward music class, computers, and CAI. In the band/orchestra group, girls were more likely than boys to want to continue using CAI.

Elementary. Intermediate-level elementary students (ages 8-10) with no prior music training who received short-term CAI in music fundamentals neither demonstrated nor retained (after a period of 112 days) a higher level of competency in fundamentals than students who received traditional classroom instruction in the same area (Dangelo, 1985).

CAI was found to be as effective as the traditional approach in teaching basic note reading to elementary students in Grades 2-4. Three modes of study were used: traditional instruction, CAI, and audio-enhanced CAI. An examination of the effect of sound incorporated into drill-and-practice routines used by elementary students in Grades 2-4 revealed no significant differences in achievement between students who used audio-enhanced CAI (pitches sounded with visual displays) and those who used the same CAI with no sound (Isaak, 1988/1989).

CAI was more effective than the traditional group approach in developing third-graders' music reading skills, and a structured CAI lab experience was more effective than untimed work. The children received a sequence of six lessons emphasizing reading skills of staff, pitch, and duration identification followed by one of three modes of practice: untimed work at the computer, a 30-minute weekly scheduled computer lab period, or regular group reinforcement. The most significant gains with this age group were with staff and duration identification (Hesser, 1988).

Fourth graders who used computer drill to learn bass clef notes scored higher in identifying bass clef notes and placing them on the staff than did those students who received drill by the teacher in the classroom. The children, classified as field dependent (students who accept learning material as presented), field independent (students who restructure learning material in their own way), or not classified, received drill in two 15-minute sessions either from a drill-and-practice CAI program or from a teacher. Field independent children showed greater achievement in identifying notes and placing them on the staff, and there was no evident interaction among field independent/dependent classification and mode of instruction (Willett & Netusil, 1989).

Teacher Tip

Use CAI drill-and-practice programs to speed the process of learning to read musical notation.

Pre-Elementary. Children, ages 4, 5, and 6, who received a 15- to 20-minute CAI lesson in addition to regular weekly classes (14 weeks) in the Yamaha Music Education System (YMES) Primary One Course showed greater improvement in pitch, rhythm, and keyboard orientation areas of the YMES program than did children who received only the regular weekly class (Bailey, 1989/1990). CAI materials incorporated the objectives of the YMES Primary One Course.

Handicapped. Students with handicaps, ages 10 to 18, who used CAI (150 minutes a week for 2 weeks) showed greater achievement in rhythm concepts than those who did not use CAI and also showed a more positive attitude toward music. For this group of handicapped students, there was also a significant correlation between attitude toward music and achievement in rhythm concept development (Isler-Hamilton, 1989/1990).

Ear training: Interval identification, melodic, harmonic, and rhythmic dictation, and sight-reading

Higher education. College students who used CAI drill in instrument identification for one month showed no greater ability to aurally identify instruments than students who received traditional instruction in instrument identification, but the author did conclude that such an application was feasible (Watanabe, 1981/1982).

A CAI approach was a more efficient method of delivery than the classroom approach for visual error detection in college-level instrumental music methods. The classroom group found some of the instruction tiring or boring, while the computer group did not. Frustration was countered in the classroom group by human interaction, while the computer group commented that such interaction would have benefited them. An optimal configuration would combine the efficiency of CAI with the interaction of the classroom (Sanders, 1980).

College choral ensemble members who worked on melodic dictation software (3 nonconsecutive 15-minute periods per week), in addition to attending choral rehearsals, demonstrated no greater sight-singing ability as a result of practice with the CAI program than did those students who had no practice with the CAI. Despite the lack of significant improvement in sight-singing skills, the researcher cited benefits that included student independence and interest in other CAI experiences (Platte, 1981).

Students in second-semester freshman ear-training instruction who used CAI harmonic dictation materials (30 minutes per week for 5 weeks) achieved higher short-term and long-term gains than did students who practiced with taped dictation materials (Garton, 1981/1982).

For college freshmen in music theory who were drilled on intervals "in a cumulative format" during a period of 8 weeks, CAI was found to be less effective than the traditional in-class approach for aural-visual interval recognition. The researcher suggested that elements of human interaction may be important in acquiring this skill. He found students' attitude toward ear training was not more favorable when CAI was used, suggesting that students may find isolated drills irrelevant, and recommended a comparison of group instruction with group instruction supplemented by CAI (Shannon, 1982).

College music students who used supplementary CAI materials in two 20-minute sight-reading lessons per week for 10 weeks demonstrated greater improvement (scoring significantly higher on a sight-reading test) than students who practiced "routinely" during the same time. The materials were designed to reinforce melodic memory, increase the number of notes perceived as a unit, provide a rhythmic context for sight-singing, and encourage the practice of reading ahead (Lemons, 1984/1985).

College freshmen in a remedial music theory class who attended three classes per week and practiced all ear training independently using a "multimedia learning sequence" (CAI, TAP tapes, and a programmed music theory manual) demonstrated achievement comparable to students who attended 5 weekly classes and received traditional instruction in ear training. While both approaches proved effective, CAI may be presumed to be more efficient since the CAI group's scores were achieved with less class time and less teacher intervention (Bowman, 1984).

College-level music students who used two different sequences of aural interval identification drills (one based on a widely used ear training text, and the other approach developed by the researcher) showed equivalent overall achievement in aural interval identification although some differences were noted during the drills (Konecky, 1986/1987).

First- and second-year college music majors who used individual drill with the TAP Master 15 minutes per day for 6 weeks, in addition to classroom instruction in sight-singing, showed greater improvement in sight-singing proficiency than did those students who received regular traditional instruction in sight-singing. The author observed that their improvement was not affected by previous sight-singing ability level, by years in college-level music, or by vocal or instrumental ensemble experience (Parker, 1979/1980).

In an attempt to provide a learning tool for sight-singing, Kolb (1984/1985) developed hardware and software for real-time pitch detection that detected and displayed sung pitches. While formal results of the tool, used by college freshmen in music theory classes, were inconclusive, the system was considered potentially useful for developing sight-singing skills. Several systems of this type are now available commercially.

College music students who worked individually with one such system, the Pitch Master, for the last 20 minutes of their regular classroom instruction (2 sessions per week for 7 and one-half weeks) showed higher levels of achievement, regardless of initial ability level, than did those students who had classroom sight-singing training during the same 20 minutes (Goodwin, 1990/1991).

In an effort to gain insight into rhythmic performance, one author wrote a computer program for use with a commercial voice processor that would simulate human evaluation of MIDI-recorded sight-singing performances by college music faculty evaluators. Since the computer program detected some performance errors that the human judges did not perceive, it might be valuable to explore use of such a program to improve instruction in sight-singing (Lorek, 1990/1991).

College students in first-semester solfège who entered with low scores showed higher achievement when placed in a traditional class situation with a teacher than when placed in a class in which a third of the time was spent working on CAI drills. Students who met for three weekly classroom sessions scored higher at midterm than students in an experimental group that used a computer drill program one day per week in addition to two weekly class meetings. By the final exam, both groups scored similarly. A comparison of placement test results and final test scores of both groups revealed dramatic differences, however. Students with initially high scores performed equally well in all categories examined (interval identification, singing intervals, and sight-singing) in the experimental and in the control group. Students placed in the CAI group who had entered with low scores achieved lower scores in all categories (Ozeas, 1992).

Secondary. Junior high trombonists (all males) who received aural/oral training according to the theory of Edwin Gordon, in combination with practice on TAP's Pitch Master during one semester, developed better pitch discrimination than did a control group. The results showed that the program was effective for improving accuracy in trombone performance (Brick, 1985).

Eighth-grade computer students who used a computer game designed to develop pitch-matching skills (speed and accuracy in detecting and correcting out-of-tune notes) 25 minutes a day for 10 days made significant gains within their group but did not show greater improvement than a group that did not use the program (Glass, 1986). The researcher acknowledged that these results were due to research design limitations and other characteristics of the study.

Secondary/Elementary. Students in Grades 4, 6, 8, and 10 who worked on a CAI program (2 half-hours a week for 8 weeks), in addition to regular classroom music instruction, and students who received only the classroom instruction showed similar gains in tonal memory, and no differences in gains were noted among the grade levels. Drake and Gaston tests, however, showed a significant difference in favor of the experimental group, and the author concluded that CAI is a feasible method for improving tonal memory (Robinson, 1984).

Students, ages 11 to 14, who used a researcher-developed CAI package with focus on tempo as an organizing cue in music listening demonstrated significant achievement in determining whether the tempo of selected patterns and melodies changed and, if so, whether it increased or decreased. Most students thought the program was fun, interesting, and helpful in understanding tempo (Turk, 1984/1985).

Sixth-, seventh-, and eighth-grade violin and viola students in their second through fourth years of study who used a tutorial and drill program for violin and viola fingering and pitch matching showed significantly higher gains in pitch discrimination achievement than did a control group that did not use the program. The CAI group practiced with the drills over a period of 3 weeks, with each student progressing through the program three times during that period. It was suggested that pitch perception would be improved if this kind of program was incorporated into a traditional program and that, if such a program were used extensively, it might have a positive effect on performance (Eisele, 1985/1986).

Elementary. Tonal memory/aural discrimination skills in first-grade students can be improved through small-group instruction and CAI. After 8 weeks of instruction in one of three groups, first-grade students in all three groups demonstrated similar achievement in tonal memory/aural discrimination skills. The approaches were divided weekly as follows: (a) 70 minutes of regular classroom music instruction, (b) 50 minutes of regular classroom music instruction plus 20 minutes of special teacher-directed activities, and (c) 50 minutes of regular classroom music instruction plus 20 minutes of CAI. Although none of the instructional approaches emerged as superior for teaching tonal memory/aural discrimination skills, the CAI group showed the most consistent growth. The author concluded that tonal memory/aural discrimination skills can be improved through use of supplementary CAI in the elementary music classroom (Whiston, 1986/1987).

Third-grade and sixth-grade students who worked in the music lab (30 minutes, 4 days per week for 6 weeks) on either the Pitch Master or the TAP Master, in addition to attending a regular general music class one day per week, showed no significant differences in achievement from students who worked in the traditional way. The author implied difficulties with schedule conflicts and suggested a closer integration of these technologies with students' previous musical experience and with current experiences in vocal/general music (Buck, 1991).

Teacher Tip

Individualize ear-training routines by "prescribing" the software and other technologies appropriate to each student's needs.

Error detection

Higher education. Opinions and perceptions of student CAI users can provide valuable insights that music educators should consider when planning to integrate CAI into the curriculum. College students enrolled in sophomore music theory who had been exposed to both computer-based melodic dictation instruction and classroom instruction gave generally positive reviews to hardware and software, but an overall negative attitude was based on their perception that the CAI required too much time in addition to class work and that too much progress was expected in too little time. They also felt a lack of consistency in the progression through difficulty levels throughout the program (Pembrook, 1986).

CAI can be effective in developing skill in pitch and rhythm error detection in college music education majors. Students in instrumental conducting or methods classes practiced with a computer program featuring four-part examples of published band literature in an interactive, programmed-instruction format. Students who used the program showed gains similar to those of students who worked in the conventional manner (Deal, 1983/1984).

Undergraduate conducting students who participated in a 9-week harmonic intonation training program, which included comparison of in-tune and mis-tuned examples, identification of type and location of intonation errors, and altering mis-tuned examples, showed greater achievement in ability to judge harmonic intonation than students who did not use the program. The groups did not differ significantly in accuracy of judging the sharpness or flatness of mis-tunings, and their achievement in harmonic intonation discrimination was not correlated with skill in harmonic analysis (Dalby, 1989/1990).

Preservice instrumental music educators who practiced error detection skills in score reading using a researcher-designed computer-based system (CAI, random-access audio, and printed music score examples) showed significant achievement gains in articulation/style and ensemble segments of the program, with the largest increase occurring in the fifth session of study. The author concluded that the system could be an effective tool in undergraduate conducting and methods classes (Jones, 1990/1991).

Students who used an interactive videodisc program designed to teach visual diagnosis of beginning trombone performance problems (posture, hand grips, embouchure, and slide technique) found that use of full-color motion sequences and overlays of computer-generated text were beneficial for learning these skills. The author concluded that the results support use of Level III computer-based interactive videodisc instruction as a supplement to traditional instruction in instrumental techniques (Atwater, 1991/1992).

Performance skills

Research in performance skills includes studies at all levels, elementary through college, involving supplementary CAI targeted at learning instrumental fingerings and improving intonation. At the college level, experimental programs of independent study for developing conducting skills and various instrumental performance skills have been implemented; technologies used include CAI and videotape. Other recent work includes interactive multimedia approaches to musical interpretation and to instrumental procedures such as reed-making.

Higher education

A group of beginning guitar students (college-level nonmusic majors) who were taught guitar tuning skills through a combination of CAI and teacher-based approaches, in addition to the regular group lesson, tuned with greater accuracy when they received computer-assisted visual feedback than when they received verbal-aural teacher feedback. The tuning instruction, however, produced no statistically significant difference in achievement in overall tuning accuracy (Codding, 1985/1986).

Hamilton (1988/1989) developed an instructional videotape program and workbook to illustrate basic performance techniques for accessory percussion instruments (bass drum, tambourine, triangle, cymbals, tam-tam, finger cymbals, wood block, and temple blocks). The materials included a separate unit for each instrument with basic information about the instrument, discussion, demonstration, and a summary exercise through which the user could try the techniques demonstrated. The video was intended for percussion students with at least one year of experience and for use as a reference tool.

Videotaped modeling can be an effective approach in beginning conducting instruction. Beginning college conducting students who used guided or unguided videotaped modeling of basic conducting skills (posture and baton position, preparatory beat, rebound, releases, and legato styles) as a supplement to regular classroom instruction in conducting demonstrated similar achievement in videotaped performance tests. The unguided modeling consisted of demonstrations of the five skills using a visual model; the guided version consisted of the same demonstrations, but was accompanied by detailed verbal instructions. Students watched the videotapes and modeled their conducting on the demonstrations (Leppla, 1989/1990).

College music students in a beginning conducting class who used computer-based interactive videodisc instruction as a supplementary learning tool achieved superior results in baton technique, cueing, musical communication, and interpretation over those who used score study and audiotape recordings (Fry, 1992/1993).

Teacher Tip

Explore the potential of video for observing and practicing conducting and other performance skills.

In an effort to help music educators provide their students with an enriched musical education that incorporates new technologies, one author developed and tested an instructional manual intended for independent study about MIDI wind controllers. The instructional materials, intended for instrumental music educators, focus on commercial wind controllers and the technical skills needed to play them, and supply ideas for integrating these instruments into the music curriculum. Goals and objectives for the project and a sequence of instructional tasks were included (Van Scoyoc, 1991/1992).

Callahan (1986) measured the speed with which students could accurately perform fingering patterns (two-, three-, and four-note patterns) derived from popular methods books. By using a clarinet and a trumpet modified with micro-switches that transmitted electronic signals to a computer, he accurately and precisely measured finger dexterity of beginning college woodwind and brass instrumentalists. He also found that the fingering patterns commonly taught to beginning woodwind and brass instrumentalists are hierarchical.

Higgins (1981) applied computer-assisted techniques to beginning clarinet study. Seventeen music education majors worked through 147 exercises and instructional materials presented by microcomputer over a period of 8 weeks. A majority of the students met most of the performance criteria. The students reacted positively toward individualization and toward the motivational aspects of the program, but none preferred computer-assisted instruction over traditional instruction.

Secondary

Secondary-school wind instrumentalists who used an interactive multimedia program that focused on tempo, dynamics, articulation, indication of form, simple ornamentation, and special effects showed significant differences in achievement in interpretive aspects of wind instrument notation in comparison to a group of students who did not use the program. Students listened to professionally recorded audio examples played on their own instruments and were to imitate these models by playing back what they heard. Enhancements that might increase the effectiveness of the program include optical storage, interactive video, and direct-to-disk recording (Adams, 1989/1990).

Secondary-school instrumental music students who used a commercially available CAI rhythm program (40 minutes per week for 6 weeks), in addition to their regular music instruction, and students who received the regular instruction with no additional study performed similarly on a tape-recorded posttest regardless of mode of study (CAI or traditional) or initial score (low, middle, or high) on a rhythm reading test (Ortner, 1990/1991).

Ninth-grade beginning clarinet students who attended individual CAI practice sessions (30-minute sessions for 10 weeks), in addition to their regular music class, and those who received only the regular music class instruction demonstrated similar performance achievement in tone quality (Malave, 1990/1991). During supplementary practice, the CAI students compared their tone quality with a model tone in both aural and visual media, and they showed some evidence of improvement. One could conclude that approaches using aural-visual stimuli and feedback might be feasible for improving tone quality performance at the ninth-grade level.

Elementary

Fourth- and fifth-grade beginning trumpet students who worked individually on a CAI trumpet fingering program scored significantly higher than did a control group on a written test of note recognition and fingerings, and scored slightly higher on a performance test. All students received traditional small-group instruction once a week. For the treatment group, the time was divided into 20 minutes of traditional instruction followed by 10 minutes of practice with the computer program, while the control group spent the entire 30 minutes in traditional instruction (Weeks, 1987).

To facilitate flute-fingering instruction, Higgins (1992) developed a flute simulator that was connected to an Apple II computer and an instructional program that randomly presented notes across the flute range. Seventh- and eighth-grade students who practiced with the flute simulator, in addition to their regularly scheduled instrument lessons and band rehearsals, achieved significantly greater gains than did students who had instrument lessons and band rehearsals only. He suggests the use of MIDI instruments as an alternative to further development of simulators.

Kassner (1992/1993) combined music CAI with mastery learning and cooperative learning in an effort to discover the combined effects on playing abilities and attitudes of fourth- and fifth-grade beginning band students. While he found no significant gains in music knowledge and performance ability, student attitudes toward the system were positive, their time on task increased, and the rate of attrition from beginning band class decreased.

Teacher Tip

Combine "older" proven technologies with newer approaches for increased learning achievement.

Other applications

Ho (1990/1991) developed a system using gauges and wires attached to the violin and bow, an analog-to-digital converter, and a microcomputer to collect, display, and store on-line information about important aspects of violin tone production (bow pressure, bow velocity, bow position, and sounding point) while the violin is played. The system allowed comparison of performances by different players: experts and novices. It could be developed into a tool for teaching tone production, could be a useful enhancement of human instruction, and could provide assistance for students between lessons with a teacher.

Interactive video applications in instrumental music can be developed at reasonable cost by refocusing existing materials, and these materials can provide an effective means of instruction. One author, using existing materials, designed an interactive videodisc application to teach oboe reed-making and evaluated the project using documentation of the procedures as well as formative evaluation. Over a period of 2 weeks, students, some of whom had never made an oboe reed, worked in groups of two or three on five different occasions. The reeds made by students using the videodisc program were judged to be similar to those made under teacher guidance (Miller, 1987/1988).

Creativity

Studies in the category of creativity include those that utilize a computer environment or microworld as an arena for compositional activities in the classroom and experiments targeted at development of hardware and software tools for composers. The instructional kinds of studies are at present concentrated at the elementary and secondary levels; they involve integration of the computer as central to classroom activities as well as the use of tool software, such as music notation programs. While these studies may be considered curriculum design projects and while they emphasize a new role for the computer, their primary focus is on the creative process.

Composers at any level

Input by means of a mouse, a peripheral device, can be interpreted as visual gesture by an appropriate computer program and can then be used to generate systems-exclusive messages in real-time as standard MIDI files; this provides the composer with greater flexibility in the use of MIDI devices. One author designed such a program, providing greater access to the internal processes of the MIDI device, and allowing access to and alteration of almost every parameter of a MIDI device through systems-exclusive messages (Nelson, 1989/1990). Many commercial sequencing programs now incorporate this technique.

Teacher Tip

Liberate the creative process by using gesture-based technologies for musical input.

Secondary

The computer can be a valuable tool for efficient music learning in a group setting, and it can be used as an integral part of the general music curriculum at the seventh-grade level. With Edwin Gordon's Music Learning Theory as the basis of instruction, Nelson (1988/1989) used the computer to teach composition and orchestration in a group setting, developing sequential lesson plans that emphasized acquisition of skills in performing, reading, and music writing within a twelve-week general music course, with the computer as the primary means of achieving the goals. This approach was intended to foster musical understanding and achievement within each student's capacity.

Computer-assisted instruction can be an effective approach in a music listening course at the secondary school level, as well as a way to apply and evaluate problem-solving skills in music composition. Mee (1988/1989) integrated a composition package into the tenth-grade music curriculum and into the tenth-grade science curriculum in a unit on the physics of sound. The overall effectiveness of the program was confirmed in both cases through study of videotapes and questionnaires. In the music composition setting, the program promoted development of creative behaviors and encouraged students to revise their ideas more extensively. This study can serve as a model for integrating microworlds into existing curricula in other disciplines (Mee, 1988/1989).

Secondary/Elementary

The LOGO Music Version language has potential as a powerful means to develop individualized music instruction. Meckley (1985) developed highly individualized computer-based music learning sequences using the LOGO Music Version language and assessed their appropriateness for students at ages 9–18, including gifted, nonhandicapped, and handicapped learners. Using this language, children formed their own microworlds of complex cognitive structures through experimentation with musical materials. Students created original compositions, developed programming skills, and explored metric, tonal, and harmonic concepts. The researcher emphasized the need to provide a balance in the interaction among student, computer, and instructor.

Elementary

Use of computer software has potential to enhance creativity, and it can contribute to an experiential understanding of music for middle school students. Fifth- and sixth-grade students who used a commercial music notation program for a total of 10 half-hour lessons during a two-and-one-half month period showed greater gains than a control group in the criterion areas of global texture, melody contour, abstraction, and closure (Conant, 1988). This author also provided anecdotal data that revealed a number of advantages of a computer environment in music education (these are found in the section on the role of the computer).

Teacher Tip

Jump over traditional hurdles of music reading and performance skills by choosing notation software that accepts MIDI input.

Davidson (1990) found that computers as compositional tools in the general music classroom (Arts Propel Program) can empower students lacking highly developed music reading and performance skills. Using appropriate notation software, students can discover and explore musical relationships by creating, playing back, and revising their own melodies.

Curriculum design

Individual uses of computer-assisted instruction as supplementary work in music reading, ear training, sight-singing, performance, and creativity have been implemented at all educational levels from pre-elementary through college. Some researchers, however, have integrated the computer into the entire curriculum, not as a supplement but as the primary means of teaching and learning. Efforts to implement these curricula have often provided insights into the techniques and procedures most likely to succeed.

Certain generally applicable human and machine problems can thwart the success of an otherwise effective educational innovation and should be considered by any teacher attempting to integrate CAI into the curriculum at any level. Computer work must be required; teachers must reorganize the course curriculum to accommodate integration of computer work and must rethink their teaching styles. Software and hardware must provide appropriate guidance, good sound quality, an encouraging grading system, and must be robust. Failure to account for these conditions may hinder integration of the computer into the curriculum and result in little impact of the computer on student learning (Bresler, 1987/1988).

Higher education

The power of the computer might be better exploited by programs such as the one developed by Kuyper (1981/1982): a CAI program in fundamentals of music theory that interrelated drill-and-practice modules with programmed learning and tutorial modules and also included study modules in many subject areas of written theory. The program was designed to accommodate new modules and to serve as a structure for integrating different teaching systems, for example, tracking student performance and using the information as a basis for future content for that student (Kuyper, 1981/1982).

Another author (Wilson, 1981) designed a sequence of CAI programs in music fundamentals (rhythm, melody, harmony, and terms) intended for nonmusic majors in elementary music methods courses. The programs, in question-and-answer format, used randomly selected questions, gave a score after each run, and used graphics. This researcher promoted awareness of the state of technology and of research on CAI in music and, while she did not test the programs, she recommended carefully documented feasibility studies (Wilson, 1981).

Multi-image, multimedia techniques are effective and appropriate for teaching music and related arts to undergraduate nonmusic majors in a music literature course (Gates, 1984/1985). Students who worked with modules designed to eliminate separation of knowledge into individual disciplines and to remove cultural filters that may inhibit the aesthetic response indicated awareness of their cultural filters and demonstrated increasing aesthetic responses in successive modules. The modules, which were based on major cultural trends and on works of individual composers and artists, used examples of music and contemporary arts from the Medieval, Renaissance, Baroque, Classical, and Romantic periods and from the twentieth century. Narrated scripts were mixed with a sound track of appropriate music, and relevant visuals were added. Similar results can be achieved now by interactive videodisc programs.

Commercially available elementary and intermediate level CAI can be successfully correlated with a commercial piano methods library. Banks (1990) coordinated a sequence of musical concepts as presented in the piano series; a description of 25 computer programs with regard to activities, ability ranges, and so on; and charts that integrate CAI with the series. She achieved this goal using minimal hardware: a computer, a monitor, a DAC (digital to analog converter) board, and a 5.25 inch floppy disk drive. The curriculum was not tested, but this model could be applied to different brands of computers and other piano methods. It could be extended to preschool and college, and MIDI in the private studio could be explored.

> **Teacher Tip**
>
> *Integrate technology into your curriculum by correlating CAI programs with your instrumental method books.*

A computer music station and music educational software can be effective resources on which to base a comprehensive violin curriculum that promotes musical literacy and understanding by involving students actively in composition, performance, improvisation, listening, and critical analysis. Strange (1990/1991) developed such a program that included songs with electronic accompaniments, coordinated theory lessons, and suggested software programs. Since the program merged new technologies with traditional practice, the researcher believes it updates the materials and adds a new dimension to violin study. After testing (4 weeks with 5 students) and evaluation (instructor, student, and parent evaluations), the curriculum was revised into a final version.

> **Teacher Tip**
>
> *Make technical practice enjoyable with MIDI "Music Minus One": sequence interesting accompaniments for scales and other technical exercises.*

Renfrow (1991) developed a sequence of objectives designed to instruct graduate piano pedagogy students in the use of computer and keyboard technology, including tasks related to operating hardware and software, and teaching applications relevant to various types of equipment. Additionally, he interviewed piano pedagogy and industry experts for suggestions for implementing the objectives and recommendations for hardware, software, and readings.

HyperCard can be used to create programs that meet the needs of many music curricula. As an illustration of the adaptability of the HyperCard environment, one author developed software (using Hypertalk) in various formats including games, tutorials, and creative reading activities for use in the keyboard curriculum. MIDI capability was used, allowing the software to utilize electronic pianos and synthesizers for input and output (Rodriguez, 1991/1992).

Secondary

Multimedia can be used to combine percussion and musicianship training. Gill (1988/1989) developed a videotaped timpani method with supplementary CAI. Designed for use with middle school and junior high students, the method consisted of 12 lessons on basics of timpani playing. Accompanying the text were videotapes of the 12 lessons, and a program for CAI in ear training was also included; the method was not tested.

Nelson (1991) describes the development and pilot testing of a seventh-grade general music curriculum (12 week, exploratory general music course) using CAI. The computer was selected as a major tool in order to help students acquire skills necessary to perform, read, and write music.

Elementary

Use of a CAI-based music curriculum in a church choir setting can improve choristers' basic musicianship, enhance the director's rehearsal effectiveness and efficiency, and provide assistance to the choir in rehearsal and performance. Participating in a researcher-developed CAI program for children's choirs in a church setting, the students matched pitch, echoed tonal and rhythm patterns, read tonal and rhythm patterns, determined melodic direction, identified songs, and used computer-based accompaniment sequences (Skelton, 1988/1989).

Computer use in the public schools is growing. In a survey of 15 K–8 public school music educators (from five school districts) who use computers in their classrooms, Syal (1992) found that while music teachers use computers in classroom and lab settings both during and outside of class time, they prefer having the computers in the classroom so that they can use them with electronic instruments. The electronic instrument of choice for this sample was the keyboard, which teachers are using in piano labs and in the general music class. Keyboards are also used to teach composition. From the information gained, Syal designed procedures for systematic

Teacher Tip

To optimize the educational power of the computer, use computers in the classroom as regular teaching tools. Place computers in the classroom itself to promote and facilitate effective instructional use.

integration of computers into the music classroom, including a timetable as well as recommendations for hardware and software selection, for funding, and for motivating students.

Testing

Much recent activity is taking place in the area of testing. The computer can provide an effective environment for measuring musical ability of very young children as well as facilitate testing of more sophisticated musical tasks.

Multiple levels

A new assessment model, computerized adaptive testing, employs artificial intelligence techniques in order to reduce time constraints, reduce examinee fatigue, and improve accuracy across differing ability levels. Vispoel and Coffman (1992) compared the efficiency, reliability, and concurrent validity of scores from a newly developed adaptive tonal memory test to scores from commercially available tests (sections of Gordon AMMA, Wing, and Drake tests). They found that the new test required an average of 71% fewer items to yield scores with greater reliability and validity than those from the Wing Tonal Memory Test. Examinees' attitudes also were significantly more favorable toward the adaptive test than toward the pencil-and-paper tests.

Peters (1992) reports developmental research that included the following goals: (a) create a computer testing station capable of judging performance accuracy of music singing (pitch and rhythm), and (b) collect data on student music performance using the station. He developed very sophisticated hardware that allows students to sing into a microphone that is interfaced with a DOS-based computer. Student performances were evaluated by means of the computer and appropriate software. Peters (1992) concluded that the package was a very valuable tool in assessing music performance data.

A test of vocal pitch-matching skill that uses a computer and MIDI hardware with microphone input was developed and tested with entering college music students. This instrument was designed to study possible relationships between pitch matching and selected performance skills, admissions criteria, previous music experiences, and personal characteristics. It revealed that pitch-matching skills were significantly related to aural-skills performance, gender, and score on the aural-skills entrance exam. Because of its accuracy and affordability, the test was recommended as appropriate for use at elementary, high school, and college levels (Etmektsoglou, 1992/1993).

Higher education

Acoustic instruments (clarinet and trumpet) modified with micro-switches that transmit electronic signals to a computer can be used to precisely measure finger dexterity of beginning woodwind and brass instrumentalists. Callahan (1986) used modified instruments to determine the speed with which beginning college wind players can accurately perform a fingering pattern and concluded that the fingering patterns commonly taught to beginning woodwind and brass instrumentalists are hierarchical.

The computer can be effective as a tool for delivering and recording test information designed to evaluate processes of formal operational thought used by 18- to 22-year-old music and nonmusic majors in listening to music. The computer can be used to analyze their listening strategies in terms of centration or decentration, and to analyze their learning style preferences for completing certain aural musical tasks. Hiranpradist (1986/1987) developed and tested a program to accomplish these goals and concluded that this type of musical analysis is a challenge to both music and nonmusic majors; information about their listening style preferences may have implications helpful to the improvement of music instruction.

HyperCard software can be used to create a computerized diagnostic test to measure the music theory achievement of entering college freshmen, to provide statistical data on that information, and to predict future success in music theory. Administration of the test, data storage, test result printouts, and statistical analysis can all be performed by the computer. Colman (1990) created and implemented a test that included 90 multiple-choice questions covering all content areas of the first-semester music theory course. He correlated test performance over a period of three college terms with theory lab grades, final percentage grades, and grade points, as well as with a three-term average for all students who completed the entire first-year theory sequence. He concluded that the test showed sufficient potential to warrant developing it as a diagnostic/predictive tool.

Secondary/Elementary

A HyperCard environment can improve evaluation of music achievement of students in Grades 4 through 11. Using HyperCard to access audio CDs, to store and display digitized music, and to synthesize music, Venn (1990/1991) created a test that measured melody, rhythm, texture, and tonality. Examinees were to indicate if a change in the element had occurred, the existence of a compositional device related to the element, and the location of the change. A format that allowed them to compose a melody for a poem was also created. Examinees controlled the playing of examples in this untimed test. Venn computed reliabilities and other relationships; the results supported the effectiveness of this test.

Elementary

By saving performance data through MIDI, one can evaluate performance and investigate theories of motor musical ability. Brotz (1990) used this approach to test the performance of three pianistic tasks that had the same timing pattern but differed in key-finding and fingering. He wanted to determine the similarity of the tasks and to identify performance proficiency at age 7, 9, and 11 years in male and female subjects playing either with right or left hand. Playing on an electronic piano interfaced with an Apple IIe computer, students learned in a half-hour lesson to play a folk song in three ways: (1) tapping the rhythm with one finger on one key, (2) tapping the rhythm with one finger on the keys needed to play the melody, and (3) using all five fingers of one hand to play the melody in rhythm. All data were saved through MIDI and examined in light of theories of motor musical ability. Brotz found performance to be slower and more inaccurate for younger subjects, for male subjects, and for more complex tasks, with left-handed performance of the most complex task more inaccurate and slower.

Pre-Elementary

Forsythe (1984/1985) designed software to deliver an adapted version of Gordon's Primary Measures of Music Audiation; she shortened the test and changed the response mode to one she found more effective than the original mode for preschool examinees. One such adaptation involved a response to the question "which one is not like the others?" rather than to "which two go together?" Forsythe found amount of training to be significantly related to musical ability, with stabilization of musical aptitude at about age 10. Children who participated in musical activities during their preschool years stabilized at higher levels.

A computer with a touch screen may afford a more appropriate method of testing musical perception (pitch discrimination and categorization) in young children, ages 3 through 5, because it helps to overcome problems of perceptual focus (in this case, pitch set and first note) by offering the opportunity for nonverbal response and for repeating the examples (D. J. K. White, 1989/1990).

A computerized test can be used to analyze the effectiveness of note presentation formats (the order in which written notes are presented) used in commercial piano methods and 4- to 6-year-old children's ability to learn note-reading skills. After 7 weeks' study using various piano methods, students were tested by means of an author-designed computer program that analyzed accuracy and response times (Lomax, 1990/1991). Lomax found no significant differences between the piano methods examined, the skill levels of the students, the most easily recognized notes, or the response times for the students tested.

Role of the computer and electronic instruments

More recent research in music technology has been focusing on exploration of the role of the computer and electronic instruments. Computer environments, microworlds that actively involve students in creative activities, are projected as the future of computing in music education. One way to create such an environment is through integration of tool software, such as music notation packages, into the curriculum to teach composition and to actively involve students in the creative process, as detailed in the section on creativity.

General

On the basis of past changes, Winteregg (1987) suggests that the symphony orchestra of the future will be a smaller hybrid organization incorporating both traditional instruments and new technologies. Positive changes of the past included replacement and addition of instruments to the orchestra. Winteregg believes that the future viability of the orchestra is linked with the capability of composers to initiate positive change in the orchestra as was the case in the past.

The future role of the computer in education is likely to be quite different from its present one. Kozerski (1988/1989) finds increasing evidence that current music education software in drill-and-practice format is neither stimulating nor necessary, and supports musical microworlds in which students are actively involved in creative exploration through compositional activities. This new role will feature computer environments for music founded upon compositional activities and an expanded role for experiential inquiry.

Elementary/Secondary

Music educators may need to incorporate electronic instruments into music programs as a complement to the existing program rather than as a replacement for acoustical instruments. Holton (1990/1991) discovered that children in Grades 3, 5, and 7 (middle to upper class, mostly white) prefer to listen to synthesized timbre more than acoustical timbre. Experience playing an instrument had a significant effect: children who played instruments tended to express greater preference for acoustical timbre while nonplayers tended to prefer synthesized timbre. The order of preference was synthesized timbre, then band instrument timbre, with string instrument timbre least preferred. Girls favored acoustical timbre and boys favored synthesized timbre. One could conclude that in the future children might prefer to play synthesized rather than acoustical instruments. Since the synthesizer's main attribute is its wide variety of timbres, music educators may want to create a unique place for synthesizers in existing instrumental and vocal groups.

Conant (1988) provided anecdotal evidence of advantages of a computer environment in music education. In her work with middle school students using a commercial music notation program, she observed that students thought using the computer was easier than playing an instrument, and the menu promoted learning of music fundamentals. The melody playback option encouraged revisions and new ideas, while simultaneous aural and visual feedback facilitated recognition of texture, melody contour, and abstraction. Finally, all students reacted positively to the computer, enjoyed using it, and wished to continue this work.

Other applications

Among the noninstructional uses of the computer in music education are management functions. There are numerous uses of general application software (word processors, data bases, spreadsheets) to complete the many administrative functions associated with music education programs.

Computerized data bases

A computer-assisted system can help music educators organize music ensemble libraries. One author designed a program that uses a data base of instrumental works listed by file number, composer, type, period, style, setting, length, solo, special features, and publisher; the program allows searches using any combination of elements (Mayson, 1982).

Telecommunications

Telecommunications is a field of increasing interest to music educators as it allows quick electronic transfer of data and creates new channels of communications. There is increasing interest in the use of electronic bulletin board services. Steinberg (1992) provides a literature review and states that computer-based telecommunications can be used very effectively for guided instruction in critical thinking. Mende (1993) lists the following bulletin boards as being of possible interest to music educators: Prodigy, Compuserve, GEnie, BIX, and Delphi. Of the large commercial services, Schopp (1993) lists Prodigy, Compuserve, GEnie, and America Online as being the most interesting to music educators.

There is particular attention placed on the bulletin board run by the music sales firm J.W. Pepper & Son; the Pepper National

Music Network (PNMN) was developed specifically for music educators and has recently included special sections relating to MENC activities (Schopp, 1993). Coan (1992/1993) developed a survey instrument to test the feasibility of using this network for survey research. He found that the respondents were overwhelmingly in favor of future surveys delivered in this way, that data retrieval was improved over other techniques, and that the quality of data was equal to the data collected by conventional means. Undoubtedly, telecommunications will be increasingly used as a research and communications tool by music educators.

Marching band drill

A comparison of the traditional approach with a computer approach to marching band show writing revealed that the computer program was not beneficial in meeting the drill writer's requirements for producing the desired show. After plotting one large and one small show, based on music, instrumentation, phrase charts, and detailed sketches using each approach, Courtney (1987/1988) found that (a) including print time, the traditional approach was faster; (b) the computer program did not allow the writer to achieve all the desired outcomes, thus interfering with the creative process; (c) the computer package did not permit plotting some forms in the desired manner; (d) animation is useful provided the required pages have been saved in memory; and (e) computer plotting is accurate to one-quarter step.

Summary

Published research provides a source through which we can gain perspective on the effectiveness of technology in music instruction and supports use of various technologies to teach a broad spectrum of music skills and concepts to students at all levels in different instructional settings and under various conditions.

Effectiveness

Some authors used commercially available CAI programs to supplement traditional instruction. At the K–12 level, they have used CAI in general music classes, band, and orchestra; at the college level, they have used CAI in music theory classes, conducting classes, music appreciation and listening courses, and music education methods classes. Earlier research was primarily directed toward supplementary CAI, which was used in addition to traditional classroom instruction.

A majority of researchers found statistically significant differences in achievement in favor of students who used CAI; others found no significant differences in achievement between CAI users and control groups. According to one perspective, this may be another way of saying that CAI is "just as good as" traditional instruction. Only a few reported that CAI was not as effective as traditional instruction.

Some researchers noted that while CAI was comparable or only moderately superior to traditional instruction, it may decrease the time traditionally required to reach the same level of achievement and it removes drill from the classroom. They have thus concluded that CAI is more efficient than traditional instruction. Some researchers observed that CAI groups showed more consistent growth. These results may be due to the Hawthorne effect, a phenomenon in which some factors (subjects' awareness that they are participating in an experiment, special procedures used) cause subjects to perform differently. This may explain the result rather than the experimental condition.

Conditions of CAI

More recently, the emphasis has been less on pitting CAI against traditional instruction and more on comparing various conditions within CAI. This is probably because teachers are convinced of the value of CAI and do not wish to deprive any students of an effective approach. Researchers have experimented with various approaches to integrating CAI into the curriculum, such as structured lab time versus untimed practice, partial class time devoted to CAI, and entire class devoted to CAI. They have experimented with differing lengths of time devoted to CAI practice. The average time spent on CAI was about two half-hour sessions per week; the duration of studies ranged from two 60-minute lessons to a full semester. People who used the TAP and Pitch Master systems usually worked in 15-minute segments.

Ability level, learning style, and attitude

Some have attempted to identify groups for whom CAI seems to work best. Variables included high, middle, or low achiever; high, middle, or low beginning proficiency level; and learning style. Handicapped and gifted students were the focus of some research. Many of the researchers noted that students showed a positive attitude toward the computer and music and, in some cases, an eagerness to continue using CAI. Some researchers provided informal or observational evidence in support of CAI.

Applications for teacher training

Research in teacher training is particularly important since ordinarily instructional innovations proceed in circular fashion (i.e., teachers tend to teach as they were taught). These researchers attempted to educate future teachers in the use of new technologies; teachers might then be expected to implement more readily some of the research findings at the K-12 levels.

Technological evolution/sophistication

Earlier experiments were directed toward use of the latest available technology in the acquisition of basic skills, beginning at the college level. Later, similar research was carried out at secondary and elementary levels. The emphasis first was on computerized drills and tutorials; later, games and simulations were added, and emphasis was placed on learning as fun rather than as a chore. While some researchers still study effects of supplementary CAI in various situations, others are experimenting with interactive multimedia and hypermedia. More significantly, they are beginning to explore a new role for the computer as central to class activities rather than continuing to study the older model of supplementary drill and practice. This computer environment, in which the computer is integral to the curriculum, is called a microworld, and is being implemented at all levels from elementary through college.

Chapter 3

Developing New Instructional Models in CAI

Theories and practice relating to instructional technology have changed significantly over time because developments have occurred rapidly. As new tools are developed, educators and researchers formulate new instructional models and applications.

Several technological applications represent possible future instructional directions: hypertext/hypermedia, artificial intelligence, robotics, and virtual reality. With the exception of hypermedia, these technologies are not yet readily obtainable for traditional classroom use. It is important, however, for educators to begin to formulate instructional models as these tools become increasingly available.

Hypertext and hypermedia

Since the late 1980s, several CAI programs in music have been developed that do not fit the traditional mold. At least in part, they allow the learner considerable freedom of navigation through the lessons and the ability to mix instructional media, including the computer, audio compact disc (CD), videodisc, and MIDI devices. Programs using CDs are being developed and used with ever increasing frequency. Although these new computer applications hold enormous potential for music teaching, these materials must be studied in order to investigate how they should be best developed and used in the music classroom.

Hypertext is an approach to information management in which data are connected by a series of links that allow nonlinear or nonsequential organization of text. The association and linking of ideas in hypertext is often compared to the associative character of human thought (Carlson, 1988; Ingraham & Emery, 1991; Jonassen, 1988, 1991; Jonassen & Wang, 1993; Nelson & Palumbo, 1992; Tripp & Roby, 1990). In recent years, the approach has been adapted for use in education; Nelson and Palumbo (1992) state that hypermedia systems in education are blossoming. Educational applications do differ in construction from those intended purely for information retrieval.

Hypermedia is simply an extension of hypertext that incorporates other media in addition to text. Hypermedia is defined as an interactive multimedia application in which discrete information units can be accessed in nonlinear ways. It is important to note that hypermedia documents are generally intended for single student use, not for use by entire classes.

Teacher Tip

Hypermedia (CD-ROM) programs are intended for individual student use.

A hypertext/hypermedia system consists of a body of information that is linked together in some type of relational manner. In most hypertext environments, and particularly in HyperCard-based applications, data are presented in pockets of information, called nodes, which contain roughly the equivalent of a 3- by 5-inch card. In hypermedia systems, this node may contain information other than text, including sound or video. The system then supports a series of links that interconnect the individual nodes. There are a number of ways in which the user can navigate through the system depending on the system organization and structure. Information may be linked in either hierarchical or referential ways, as shown in Figure 2.

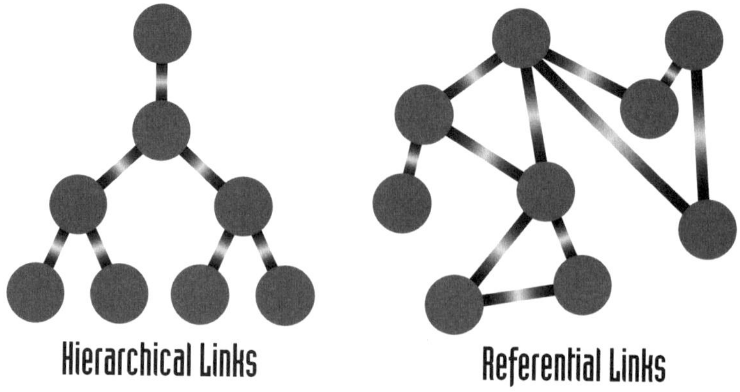

Figure 2. Relationships of hypermedia links

In most music applications using audio CDs, students listen to the music while viewing information presented on the computer screen. Students may move to related topics, unfamiliar concepts or words, and/or background information. These applications also provide a menu based on the form of the piece being studied so that students can order their listening; students are not limited to a linear presentation of the music, but may jump from section to section–a process that may disrupt the continuity of the music. The linear character of music does restrict the nonlinear approach with the result that hypermedia applications in music do differ from those in other fields. There are thus considerably more navigational restrictions in music applications than in non-musical applications.

Learning implications and learning strategies

The main purpose of any hypermedia document is to present information–a knowledge base–to the learner. It is an electronic book of sorts, in which the information presented is not limited to text and the presentation is nonlinear, allowing the user considerable freedom. It is a new, very flexible information delivery system, which eliminates the arbitrary sequencing of traditional text (Nelson & Palumbo, 1992). Jonassen (1992) stresses that hypermedia can help learners access information in order to solve problems and acquire knowledge–learners become constructors of knowledge. Because of the inherent freedom of the environment, the student must develop different strategies in order to learn from this different environment (Tripp & Roby, 1990).

Teacher Tip

Help students develop appropriate learning strategies for dealing with the unique presentation of hypermedia tutorials.

Marchionini and Shneiderman (1988) identify four broad factors in interface design that may affect the self-regulation of learning: access points, the creation of the user interface, search strategy features, and flexibility versus complexity. The first factor relates to determining what access points should be defined, how fine the access points should be, how the points should be linked, and what links should be visible to the user. Access points can follow many of the same formats found in traditional print media such as tables of content, indexes, appendixes, and reference lists. The size and nature of the node is also of concern, not only in terms of user perception but also in terms of hypertext structure. Research clearly shows that short-term working memory is limited in terms of storage; short-term memory capacity has been set to approximately seven "chunks" of information (Miller, 1956). Kearsley (1988) states that the material in each node should be organized into small "chunks" that deal with only one subject.

The second factor influencing the regulation of learning is the creation of the user interface—the ability for the user to interact positively with the machine. After actions are made, the user must receive appropriate and understandable feedback in order to maintain meaningful interaction.

The third factor deals with search strategy features. Since there is such a high degree of user freedom, students may choose radically different approaches. Users may simply browse, moving from one card to the next in a linear fashion; others may jump from area to area. There does seem to be evidence that individuals do use these documents in significantly different ways (Berz, 1991; Frey, 1989; Horney, 1993; Lanza & Roselli, 1991; Y. B. Lee, 1989; Tripp & Roby, 1990; Tsai, 1989). Either because of unfamiliarity with the environment or because of a lack of adequate prior knowledge about the subject being studied, students may choose incorrect or inappropriate search strategies given the teacher's instructional goal. Navigation concerns can be among the greatest problems in hypertext (Conklin, 1987).

Teacher Tip

With CD-ROM tutorials, provide clear objectives to learners so that their exploration of the materials can be focused.

Relative to the fourth factor—flexibility versus complexity—Conklin (1987) identifies a problem termed cognitive overhead. The user must expend cognitive energy to make the many navigational decisions that arise. Making these decisions may actually hinder memory of the material that is to be learned. Additionally, when a student is working on a tangential area, he or she may forget the primary material; again, the encoding process is confused, this time with additional, possibly irrelevant information. Tripp and Roby (1992) confirm that "concerns about the draining of mental resources by disorientation in a hypertext learning environment are justified" (p. 122).

Aside from these four factors, other learning concerns have been identified. In virtually all of the commercially available hypermedia applications in the field of music, learners are directed to read computer displays while music is playing. In related research in the field of perception and memory, Salame and Baddeley (1989) report disruptions of memory caused by background speech or music (unattended speech effect); people are not able to attend very efficiently to streams of simultaneous multiple information. This research would seem to suggest that learners might not be able to pay attention to both the music and the textual explanations, let alone consider making navigational choices. This problem is further compounded by the fact that reading text on a computer may be more difficult than reading the same text in books (Haas, 1989).

There are some advantages to having multiple sources of information available for student consideration. Researchers (Fleming, 1987a, 1987b; Levie, 1987) have found that memory for learning words is enhanced by associating pictures with the words to be memorized. It would seem only logical to assume that this concept can be carried further in associating pictures and sound to help learners form meaningful concepts in music. The ability to link musical sounds with text and graphics would seem to be of considerable value in teaching the elements of a given piece of music.

Hypertext research

Vannevar Bush (1945), President Roosevelt's science adviser, is credited with first describing the concept of hypertext in his article "As We May Think," published in the *Atlantic Monthly.* This concept was carried significantly further by Douglas C. Englebart and Ted Nelson some 20 years later. Englebart adapted Bush's ideas to the computer in the 1960s. Engelbart's goal was to provide better devices with which to think, as well as tools with which to create better tools–an augmentation of the human intellect (Fraase, 1990). During this same time period, the theory of hypertext was refined and expanded by Nelson, who actually coined the words *hypertext* and *hypermedia* (Locatis, Letoumeau, & Banvard, 1989). In 1983, Randall Trigg was the first to write a doctoral dissertation on the subject of hypertext (Conklin, 1987). The early history of hypertext is further summarized by Chen (1989), Conklin (1987), Farmer (1989), Irish and Trigg (1989), Locatis, Letoumeau, and Banvard (1989), Rada (1989), and van Dam (1988).

Although there is a rather significant body of literature related to hypertext and hypermedia, much is not empirical research. The exploratory nature of the literature is not surprising given the newness and developmental nature of the field. There are a number of bibliographical reviews of the literature (Ambrose, 1991), many of which are found in the field of library science (Franklin, 1990; Franklin & Bessmer, 1990; Lin, 1988).

One line of research investigates hypertext system use in real-life settings. One such study is by Shneiderman, Brethauer, Plaisant, and Potter (1989); it studied the use of a hypertext application in three museums. Specific questions addressed included: selections made, time spent reading the selection, access of index, abandoned sessions, duration of session, and corrected duration. In studying the use of the application in the third museum, the authors investigated other concerns including interface design in the real-world environment. The authors concluded that the hypertext application was well received by the visitors. Visitors seemed to select articles based on interest rather than on random selection; this was illustrated by navigation patterns.

Another line of research reports the development of hypertext and/or hypermedia systems as instructional tools in educational settings (Barden, 1989; Berz, 1991/1992; Burnett, 1991; Hall, Thorogood, Hutchings, & Carr, 1989; Hirsch, Kelly, &

O'Donnell, 1992). Schouten (1988/1989) developed and pilot-tested a hypertext data base structure about musicians, music, and music education. A master structure was developed by combining the relevant portions of previously identified lists and indexes, and was demonstrated as an indexing and data management tool by classifying fifty articles, research reports, and recordings.

Yet another line of research investigates various concerns encountered in this type of instruction, such as philosophical and design considerations and user attitudes. There is particular research interest concerning user navigation (search strategies, interface designs, and the study of audit trails) in hypertext and hypermedia documents (Beasley, 1992; Beasley & Vila, 1992; Fujihara, Snell, & Boyle, 1992; Kinzie & Berdel, 1990; Knuth, 1992/1993; Misanchuk & Schwier, 1992; Small & Grabowski, 1992; Stanton, Taylor, & Tweedie, 1992). Klappenberger (1990) found that prior knowledge of a given domain affected subjects' search efficiency of a hyperdocument in that domain. This was true in terms of time efficiency and correctness in answering assigned questions. Students do not necessarily take advantage of the nonlinear organization; some read the material in regular, linear ways even within large associative webs (Horney, 1993). Other research investigates searching methodology (Rada & Murphy, 1992; Shneiderman, Brethauer, Plaisant, & Potter, 1989).

There is some research investigating the effectiveness of hypermedia systems. Hughes (1991) compared two learning strategies for college music majors ($n = 80$) in developing recognition of a core music repertoire. The control group used a traditional repeated-listening strategy. The experimental group ($n = 17$) used a hypermedia approach that had been developed by the researcher. Subjects in the experimental group had significantly higher scores on a recognition posttest of composers, works, movements, and theme groups.

Teacher Tip

Hypermedia tutorials allow easy and unique manipulation of mixed media that hold great potential for music education.

Using a HyperCard stack, students rated a serial composition (after one listening) on preference, performance, complexity, and understanding (Sigurjonsson, 1991). They read a description designed to spark their thinking about the composition, wrote a response to the music, and rated the music a second time on the same four criteria. The participants rated the music differently after they wrote their response. Time spent and interactivity increased for all subjects, from freshman nonmusic majors through freshman, senior, and graduate music majors.

Goodson (1992/1993) developed a module of an interactive hypermedia program for intelligent music listening to explore the challenges faced by music educators when using this medium and to test its value as an instructional tool. The author concluded that the interactive hypermedia instruction required less instructional time than traditional methods to produce equal or higher student achievement on a 22-item test.

Hypermedia/hypertext conclusions

Following theoretical work that began in 1945, various approaches to hypertext were developed largely as a tool to manage information. Within the past few years, hypermedia has been adapted for use in education, with a number of commercial applications available in music.

Basic research in the use of hypermedia in education is just beginning. At this juncture, research comparing hypermedia instruction with traditional instruction tends to show no significant difference between the two approaches. Very often the comparison test covers the presentation of basic factual/verbal information. Hypermedia's strength is (a) providing a medium where the learner is not restrained by the structure of the learning environment, and (b) presenting information in different media, notably pictures and sound. Perhaps given the developmental nature of this technology, comparison studies might not be the best route for researchers to take; in any event, some researchers question this approach to technology research (Clark, 1983, 1985). Research must be conducted to see if and how learning takes place and, perhaps even more importantly, in what kinds of learning environments hypermedia should be used.

As is the case with any learning strategy, hypermedia is best used when the setting is appropriate. The conclusions of the Hughes (1991) study indicate that hypermedia is well suited to those situations that are not appropriate for traditional approaches. Hypermedia could be employed in settings where information is best presented in multiple modes in nonlinear ways.

Artificial intelligence

Edmunds (1988) associates artificial intelligence (AI) with those areas of computer science that attempt to duplicate certain functions performed by the human body and mind. For the psychologist and researcher, it is a field of enormous complexity, controversy, and breadth. Artificial intelligence is really a collection of different fields sharing a common goal of developing a computational model of human intelligence; writing in the field is quite diverse. McConnell and McConnell (1988) cite several major AI streams: programming, problem solving, automated reasoning, game playing, natural language (enabling a computer to understand and comprehend human language), expert systems, machine learning, robotics, and vision. Cognitive psychology has both influenced and been influenced by AI.

Expert systems

Intelligent tutoring systems (ITSs) began to be developed in the 1960s as a reaction to problems associated with ordinary CAI (Yazdani, 1987). It was felt that student responses should determine what that student would be shown next; the machine would "react" or "adapt" to the student's behavior.

Perhaps the widest use of AI is in expert systems (Frenzel, 1987). The term *expert system* is relatively new, having surfaced in the literature in 1977 (Lefrere, Waller, & Whalley, 1987). An expert system uses a knowledge base of computer-readable information representing facts and formal rules about a given knowledge domain. It is called an expert system because the knowledge and rules are obtained ordinarily by interviewing one or more experts in that field. In theory, the completed system performs about the same way that the expert would in answering an appropriately narrow class of questions. The application is, therefore, limited to those rules and facts that are actually programmed into the system.

Central to an expert system is the inference engine. An inference engine is the part of the expert system that takes the information from the user and fits it into the rules in the knowledge base in order to generate the machine's response. Some people call the inference engine a rule interpreter (Edmunds, 1988). Following some of the theories of cognitive psychologist John R. Anderson, inferences are often made based on what are called productions (see Gagne & Glaser, 1987, pp. 58-63, for a discussion of Anderson's concept of productions in human memory). Productions often follow an "if-then" rule structure. An example might be:

IF

1. the chord has three notes, *and*
2. the interval between the bottom two notes is a major third, *and*
3. the interval between the upper two notes is a minor third,

THEN

the chord is a major triad.

These productions can also use other logic chains, such as "and-or" or "when-then," in combination with the "if-then" clause. The basic structure for the development of an expert system is shown in Figure 3.

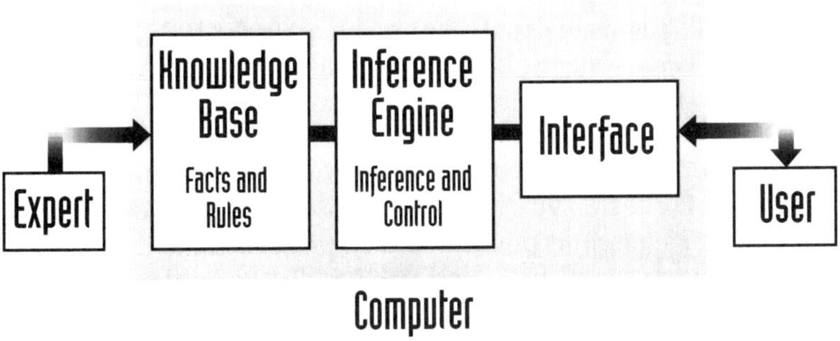

Figure 3. Components of an expert system

Expert systems are best employed in situations where there are concrete rules–not where rules are too vague to be easily translated into the "if-then" structure (Vitale & Romance, 1991). Often a shell–an organizing structure/program devoid of hard, specific information–is employed to build new expert systems in new domains; the organizing structure is, in a way, recycled into a new environment.

AI research

McConnell and McConnell (1988) credit the formulation of AI as a discipline to Alan Turing and Claude Shannon in 1950. They state that the Dartmouth Conference of 1956 is generally accepted as the date of the creation of AI as a formal science. A popular research emphasis of the 1950s was the creation of an electronic brain. The focus of 1960s research shifted more to function and away from form. Hsieh and Hall (1989) state that the first successful applications were developed in the early 1970s. The mid-1970s and early 1980s saw a partnership develop between AI researchers and other professionals, and finally in the 1980s commercial applications of AI emerged. ITSs are products of the 1980s (Rosenberg, 1987).

Two major themes are currently stressed in the research literature in AI, particularly as it relates to education: theoretical discussion and system development. There are a few studies outside of these two primary areas. One such study focuses on student learning resulting from the development of students' own expert systems (Knox-Quinn, 1988, 1991).

There is boundless discussion of human intelligence and cognition as it relates to AI; this general theoretical AI literature is vast. Burns and Capps (1988) identify the primary authors of this field: John Anderson, Kurt VanLehn, Henry Halff, Richard Burton, James Miller, William Johnson, David Littman, and Elliott Soloway.

The second body of literature details and/or describes the development of ITSs. Yazdani (1986) cites some 22 systems that were developed before 1986. Barr and Feigenbaum (1986) discuss eight systems in detail. Tennyson and Park (1987) also classify some early systems. Legree and Gillis (1991) review literature relating to the instructional effectiveness of some specific ITSs.

Developed in 1970 by Carbonell, SCHOLAR was one of the first applications of AI in education (Barr & Feigenbaum, 1986; Stubbs & Piddock, 1987); the system first attempts to diagnose the student's misconceptions and then presents materials to help the student recognize his or her error. SOPHIE, developed in the mid-1970s, was another landmark in the improvement of ITSs (Stubbs & Piddock, 1987); by restricting the domain, SOPHIE could answer most questions posed of it. Other very early systems include BIP, WHY, WEST, GUIDON, WUMPUS, BUGGY, MYCIN, and WUSOR. There is a growing body of literature that details the development of new ITSs and/or shells (Bare, 1988; Dorin, 1990; Elieson, 1990; Ford, 1987; Jacobson, 1989; Martindale, 1987; McEneaney, 1991; Palitawanont, 1989; Sener, 1991; B. A. White, 1990; Wixom, 1990).

There is some AI work in music education, largely in music theory instruction. Music theory and music analysis are fields that are particularly well suited for intelligent tutoring, because they are dominated by teaching and application of different kinds of rules. In a very early and important study, Meehan (1979) discusses theoretical underpinnings for using AI in the analysis of music. The basic orientation is drawing an analogy between musical structure and natural language processing.

Expanding on previous research (Schaffer, 1988a, 1988b), Schaffer (1991) describes the development of interrelated exploratory ITSs (provided by Schaffer's program, the *Harmony Coach*) designed to coach students in the diatonic harmonization of unfigured melodies and bass lines and in the development of part-writing skills. The author states that the tutorials contain a sufficiently large knowledge base capable of dealing with all the basic formulations relating to non-modulatory common-practice harmony. Schaffer concluded that the *Harmony Coach* does meet the above conditions with varying levels of success. He identifies some problems being addressed, such as the quality of machine response, particularly to unusual situations. As in many AI situations, responses that fall outside of the "normal" rule structure present some problems. Schaffer (1991) concludes that "despite numerous shortcomings, intelligent tutorials are proving to be a worthy successor to the previous generation of drill-and-practice CAI" (p. 35). Schaffer's work does show that ITS development is possible in a microcomputer environment in music education.

Also based on earlier research (Holland, 1986), Holland (1989) developed an AI application to encourage and facilitate music composition by musical novices. First, a music manipulation tool, *Harmony Space,* was developed based on Longuet-Higgins's theory of harmony. With this tool, novices were allowed to sketch, analyze, modify, and compose harmonic sequences by moving two-dimensional patterns on a computer screen with the computer linked to a synthesizer. From the results of a pilot study, the author found that *Harmony Space* could help musical novices perform the following tasks in a relatively short training period:

1. carry out harmonic analyses of the chord function and modulations of pieces, such as "Ave Verum Corpus" by Mozart;
2. accompany songs, playing the correct chords, on the basis of simple verbal instruction or demonstrations;
3. carry out simple strategies for composing certain chord sequences;
4. modify existing chord sequences in musically sensitive ways; and
5. play and recognize various classes of abstractly described, musically useful chord sequences in various contexts.

A second component to Holland's study was an application called *MC,* described as "something between a framework for an aural generative hypertext system and a song synthesizer" (Holland, 1989, p. 181). "The *MC* architecture promotes the use of goal-oriented, high-level strategic thinking" (Holland, 1989, p. 219). It is a knowledge-based tutoring system drawing on certain definitions of creativity.

In addition to the above systems, other ITSs in music have been identified: *Vivace* (harmonization), *MacVoice* (voice leading), *Lasso* (sixteenth-century counterpoint), *THE MUSES* (music theory), and *Piano Tutor* (Holland, 1989). Sorisio (1987) reports the development of the ITS in harmony. Several applications that employ AI were developed to assist in musical analysis or composition (Garton, 1988/1989; Harris & Brinkman, 1989; Leblanc, 1990; Maxwell, 1984/1985; Simoni, 1983). Jones, Miller, and Scarborough (1988) report the development of a rule-based expert system for music perception.

Artificial intelligence techniques have been applied to assessment using computers. Vispoel (1993a) reports the development and evaluation of a computerized adaptive test of tonal memory. The computer presents items of varying difficulty based on the subject's responses to previously presented questions. Using this approach, fewer items can be given without sacrificing reliability; this reduces the amount of time needed to administer a test. The field of adaptive testing in music is reviewed by Vispoel (1993b).

Combining AI and hypermedia

For the most part, hypermedia and AI have been developed autonomously, both having roots in noneducational settings. Little research and development has been undertaken to combine the two strategies. Midoro, Olimpo, Persico, and Sarti (1991) state that AI techniques can be used to help solve some of the navigation problems in interactive multimedia systems by providing advice and guidance to students as they search the material; the authors describe the development of such a system. Other related research includes Garg (1989) and Tang, Barden, and Clifton (1991).

Conclusions regarding artificial intelligence

Several practical problems have been identified in developing and implementing ITSs (Woolf, 1990). Most notable is the complexity encountered in developing such systems. Development of ITSs is a time-intensive activity and requires rather intensive training. Woolf (1990) states that "it appears that two person-years is a convenient estimate for practical development of these systems" (p. 242). Schaffer (1991) notes that "programming complex intelligent tutorials is simply beyond the capabilities of the average weekend programmer" (p. 35). Many systems are developed by collaborative teams (Woolf, 1991). Clearly, system development is well beyond the reach of the average educator.

Teacher Tip

Currently available artificial intelligence systems are most valuable in domains that are rule based, such as music theory. Avail yourself of this new approach.

Other practical problems include the limited number of school computers that are powerful enough to handle AI-based applications, a lack of practical applications for the school setting, general resistance for a variety of reasons, and difficulties in integrating intelligent tutors into existing curricula. Burns and Capps (1988) express concern in bringing laboratory developed ITSs into the real world. This also illustrates the point that experts may not be able to define in practical ways the path to expertise; they may have learned the elementary steps so long ago and the steps are so automated that they are not considered in the instructional model.

Even with the problems listed, artificial intelligence is the clear successor to traditional CAI; AI can move well beyond drill-and-practice methodologies and can encourage students to develop new skills and expertise. The approach has the potential to copy human teaching models; that is, AI can identify what the student already knows, develop a teaching strategy, alter the strategy based on student responses, and evaluate progress. Increasingly, computer applications in education possess intelligent characteristics to at least some degree. Unfortunately, because the field is still highly dynamic and developmental, adequate models have not been fully developed and evaluated.

Robotics

The term *robot* was first introduced in 1917 by Karel Capek in his short story "Opilec" (McCloy & Harris, 1986). Ever since Isaac Asimov coined the term *robotics* in the early 1940s, the field has been of significant interest in the popular, scientific, and industrial communities. Particularly in industry, robots have played significant roles in improving productivity or replacing human workers in certain repetitive or unsafe environments. Perhaps at some point, the discerning orchestra conductor will be able to requisition a robot bassoonist.

Robotics is a segment of the larger field of artificial intelligence. In the industrial setting, a robot is defined as a reprogrammable multifunction manipulator designed to perform some specified task(s); reprogrammability and multifunctionality are key for a device to be called a robot instead of a simple automated device (Tidewater Technology Associates, 1990). Robots have a variety of component parts including a computer, power source (electrical, hydraulic, pneumatic), manipulator, and measuring devices that may include vision (camera or the like) or other "sensory" inputs (McCloy & Harris, 1986). Robots have become increasingly popular in industry, particularly in heavy manufacturing.

Robotics development

The history of real robots began in 1954 with a patent application by American engineer George Devol; that patent led to the first industrial robot manufactured in 1962 by Unimation, Inc. (McCloy & Harris, 1986); some authors place this date as 1961 (Ashley, Konopka, & Carrico, 1983; Pawson, 1988). Most of the research in this field is technically oriented and application based.

Robots in education

Introducing robots into education requires the development of user awareness and applications. Pawson (1988) states that in overall application "robotics is in much the same position now that computing faced ten years ago" (p. 2). There is very limited work on using robots in the process of teaching or learning. There are several bibliographies (Garoogian, 1984; Kissinger, 1987) that list robotics research that might have relevance in education, and Pantelidis (1991) lists approximately 1,500 classified citations pertaining to the educational use of robots. Gray (1988) states that in 1984 there were approximately 12,000 robots in use in American secondary schools.

Robotic applications in education are most commonly found in industrial arts education (preparing for future vocations), elementary education (class activity), science education, or higher education (research and development, training for industry). Most contemporary educational applications of robots can be grouped into one of several categories: robots as exemplars of other concepts or processes, robots as objects of study, and robots as a functional aid for use with the handicapped (Post, Howell, & Rakocy, 1988). One of the most common uses of robots as exemplars is in the computer programming process; for example, the Terrapin Turtle in LOGO is often used in robotics education in the elementary classroom. The design and building of robots is receiving ever increasing attention in the popular and educational press, especially in reports related to the criticism that American schools are not preparing students for taking a place in society (Draper, Cahoon, & Clayton, 1986; Tidewater Technology Associates, 1990). There are a number of educational applications of robotics for industrial arts and science education (Ashley, Konopka, & Carrico, 1983; Keramas, 1990; Schoeffler, 1990; Schultz, 1986).

Some authors report that robots can be used to teach concepts such as problem solving (Gray, 1988) in much the same way that some computer programs (data bases, spreadsheets) are employed to teach reasoning, logic, and problem solving. Wagner (1991) investigated whether robotics, as compared to battery-powered manipulatives or traditional methods, could significantly improve science achievement scores or problem-solving scores in upper elementary students. She concluded that robotics were not more effective in this regard than the other approaches.

Conclusions regarding robotics

At present, robotics would seem to hold the least potential for music teaching of any of the "new" technologies. This is due largely to the fact that robotics technology has not been developed to the point where it can be employed in meaningful ways; development has been focused on industrial applications. One can only speculate whether robot bassoonists or robot teachers will have a place in the future.

Virtual reality

Virtual reality (VR) is a computer-created sensory environment that duplicates a real-life experience. Virtual reality systems carry the simulation concept to an extreme, placing the learner/user in a simulated reality. The Holodeck on the popular television series "Star Trek: The Next Generation" is an idealized example of virtual reality, indistinguishable from the real world. Traub (1991) describes virtual reality environments as "an ideal milieu for learning" (p. 111).

Typically, virtual reality systems have a variety of interfaces between user and machine (Spring, 1991); sometimes these kinds of systems are called immersive VR (Jacobson, 1991). The most common links include goggles or a helmet containing small computer screens for each eye; the DataGlove (produced by VPL Research), which contains tracking sensors and fiber optic strands running down each finger; and the DataSuit, which is similar to the DataGlove but has sensors accounting for motions of the entire body. The user is connected to the computer by a type of "umbilical" cord. An ideal environment would not use wire connectors and would allow the user to move within the environment unencumbered (Krueger, 1991a). Ideally, the interface between human and machine would be totally nonintrusive—a goal that is not yet technologically possible.

There are many desktop VR applications available, particularly in computer-aided design, which are not "immersive" (Jacobson, 1991). With these kinds of programs, people view and interact with a three-dimensional environment displayed on the conventional computer monitor. These applications are being employed in theatrical set design and allow users to move freely in the set before it is actually built.

Virtual reality development

Much of the theoretical foundation of virtual reality was established by Myron Krueger in his 1983 book *Artificial Reality* (Fritz, 1991; Krueger, 1991a, 1991b), which was developed from his dissertation of 1974. Krueger (1991a, 1991b) credits Ivan Sutherland (who invented the first three-dimensional, head-mounted display), Tom Furness (who developed displays, other experiments, and flight simulation), and Fred Brooks (who developed manipulators) with important early developments. In addition, "the importance of this technology coming from NASA cannot be overestimated" (Krueger, 1991b, p. 22); beginning in 1984, Michael McGreevy at NASA built upon Furness's work. Krueger also credits Nintendo for resurrecting popular interest in the technology. He cites 1989 as a turning point for the field because of the headline "What If Artificial Reality?" on the front page of the *New York Times,* which led to further media interest. Jaron Janier, chief executive officer of VPL Research, coined the term *virtual reality* in 1989 (Krueger, 1991a). Randal Walser, directing development at Autodesk, has led pioneering work in education and athletic applications (Krueger, 1991a). NASA continues important work in developing and using virtual environments (Fisher, 1991). Most notable among academic institutions conducting VR research are the University of North Carolina at Chapel Hill, the Massachusetts Institute of Technology, and the University of Washington (Newquist, 1991).

Virtual reality possibilities in arts education

Simulation strategies are used to reproduce dangerous, expensive, or unique situations or environments. Flight simulators are probably the best known example of this instruction; they are employed for the obvious reason that it is not particularly prudent to practice crash landings with a real 747. In schools, some traditional CAI simulations are available, but they are limited in scope, appeal, or effectiveness. Virtual reality suggests active participation–an experienced-based education. "Future presidents will field hostile questions from a graphic Sam Donaldson in rehearsal before they face the real thing" (Krueger, 1991, p. 189).

The possibilities of virtual simulations in music stagger the imagination. One possibility might be in teaching conducting. Students could practice conducting an imaginary, virtual orchestra, whose players would respond to every gesture. Students could perform compositions on self-developed instruments that are not bound by physical technique. Students could move to music with tempi varying according to student or instructor intent; a virtual partner could be present to complement or replay movements (as seen on a recent "Star Trek" episode). Students might discuss sonata-allegro form with Mozart. The possibilities are limitless.

Krueger (1991a) also states that the technology has significant aesthetic potential. He views it as a new medium for artistic expression. He cites several examples–visual art, dance, theater, and poetry–in which serious art was created by and in virtual environments. Although he does not discuss music specifically, the possibilities still exist.

VR technology holds special potential for the physically handicapped. In VR, students are not bound by physical restraints and may, therefore, move into environments free from physical restraints.

Conclusions regarding virtual reality

Virtual reality is the least developed of these largely untested technologies. Presently, there are few applications available for the ordinary classroom, because of technological limitations. However, from at least a theoretical standpoint, virtual reality holds great educational potential; both hypermedia and artificial intelligence are burdened by excess philosophical baggage. In robotics, the technology is being developed largely for industrial and not educational application. While still a bit of a fantasy, virtual reality will probably become more practical for educational use, maybe not in the "Star Trek" Holodeck model, but in simpler, more accessible applications.

Chapter 4

Conclusions and Summary

Educational technology is a rapidly changing field. As new technologies are developed, research strategies change and previous conclusions need to be evaluated. Even the common experimental approach of direct comparison studies (new versus old approaches) is under direct fire because of validity concerns. In addition, new instructional approaches have been and are being developed that are radically different from the thoroughly tested CAI programs of the 1970s and 1980s; findings derived from earlier research may or may not be valid for these new models. For these reasons, deriving concrete conclusions from technology research is indeed a complex and problematic task.

Teachers and researchers must, however, examine the literature as it exists in the present in order to make informed decisions on how best to help students grow and to advance the field. Certainly, older research does set the framework for new efforts and does help to determine teaching practice. New research can then help to redefine and refine teaching methods.

The following conclusions are presented for teachers to consider when employing technology in the music classroom. They are derived from an examination of the research literature presented in this book.

Integrating technology into music teaching

The research generally shows that CAI and other technologies can be effective learning tools, and the way that teachers integrate these technologies into the classroom is an essential element in their effectiveness. Some researchers attributed inconclusive or negative results achieved with CAI to problems encountered in integrating technology into the curriculum. These problems include difficulties with schedule conflicts, lack of integration of technologies with students' previous musical experience or with current experiences in vocal/general music, a need for human interaction in acquiring certain skills, irrelevance of isolated drills, a need for a more musical approach, and failure to rethink the course.

Carefully assess your teaching situation, rethinking the course, your role in the classroom, and the role of the technology you intend to use. Careful instructional planning is vital to productive teaching. TIPS: Technology for Music Educators, *an MENC publication, offers many specific, practical suggestions for teachers beginning to integrate technology into their teaching.*

Instructional choice: Special concerns

The field of instructional technology is extremely broad, including a wide variety of media, each possessing its own specific characteristics. Each kind of technology can be used with great success if it is used for its designed purpose.

Have realistic expectations and understandings about how each technology should be used for educational gain. Each media form has a specific purpose by nature of its design. Try to employ only those technologies that are suited for the educational task at hand.

Transfer

Transfer is a phenomenon that refers to the effect of previously learned information on newly learned material. Transfer can be both positive and negative; negative transfer would hinder or block new learning. Many music researchers have studied the use of CAI in developing skills that are then expected to transfer to other situations (e.g., acoustic situations).

When developing your goals, examine the nature of the musical tasks you wish to address with CAI or other technology in order to form reasonable expectations for the results. Make sure that students understand the relationship between the computer task and the material to be learned. Relate the CAI task to the other classroom activities.

Student developmental levels

Across all educational levels, there have been varied results with regard to populations for whom CAI works best and the circumstances under which it is most successful.

Consider the developmental level of the students for whom you are designing technology-related experiences and align the experiences with techniques appropriate to that age or stage. Implement CAI as one of several effective approaches, but one that warrants serious consideration because of its documented successes and because it is an approach to which contemporary students can easily relate.

Learning strategies

Learning strategies can be defined as behaviors of learners that are intended to influence how they process information. The term *strategies* also implies a possibility of learners' employing multiple or alternative ways to learn that are best for them, depending on a given situation. Specific learning strategy choice will impact immeasurably on encoding in both short- and long-term memory.

In many CAI programs, particularly in the new approaches (such as hypermedia), students are immersed in an environment with significant freedom. It is clear that the learner must develop appropriate strategies in order to learn from this setting. These strategies are possibly quite different from those employed in other, more conventional approaches, such as with books (text and pictures) and lectures. There is a tendency for students to move off task when using CAI, such as getting too involved in the gaming aspect of instructional games or moving to unrelated material in hypermedia programs.

Provide your students with guidance on how to use the computerized environment. Not only must they understand the practical workings of the equipment, but they also need help on how best to learn from the environment, just as they might need to learn how to take notes in a traditional setting. Just as in traditional instruction, make sure that your students have a clear understanding of what is to be learned so that they can best direct their efforts for successful learning.

Expertise

Novices and experts normally have different knowledge representations. Experts are distinguished in part from novices in a given domain by the nature of their mental models and how they are used to solve given problems. It has been shown that experts read conventional text in their domain differently than do novices. It is assumed then that experts and novices might use different strategies in using computer applications.

In choosing educational software, consider the previous experience of the students for whom the instruction is intended. Make sure that the content of the program relates to the expertise of the student.

Procedures

Most studies involved integration of CAI into the curriculum as supplementary instruction; ordinarily the drill and practice took place in a computer lab in which students worked independently in addition to their regular class work. A few authors substituted CAI for a scheduled class, while others have been creating a new role for the computer as central to the regular activities of the classroom. Several authors reported student frustration with requirements that were perceived as unreasonable or irrelevant and with absence of human interaction.

Substitute CAI drill sessions for one class rather than simply adding CAI to the other requirements. Prior to implementation, conduct a thorough review of the programs to be used and determine their appropriateness in your situation. Finally, combine CAI with classroom interactivity for optimum results.

Student response

Both positive and negative student responses to CAI have been documented in a number of studies. This information can be helpful to teachers planning to implement CAI.

To achieve productive implementations of technology in music instruction, observe the effect of the approach on attitude and feeling and consider how that impacts on the educational experience. Capitalize on students' natural enthusiasm for working with the computer and on their inclination to continue enjoyable activities. Students learn best when they are motivated to learn.

Implementation time

Dramatic results should not be expected of any approach used in the short term. Conclusions about the effectiveness of technological instruction should not be drawn until it has been integrated into the curriculum and has been used consistently over the long term.

After initial preparation and integration, implement the chosen technology in a consistent fashion for a time period appropriate to your goals, perhaps for one semester; then evaluate the results.

Emerging technologies

A number of technological applications represent future instructional directions: hypertext/hypermedia, artificial intelligence, robotics, and virtual reality. All have the quality of increasing the interaction between the user and the machine. Unfortunately, most of this technology has not been adapted for use in the K–12 classroom. The exception is hypermedia, for which several music applications are commercially available.

Combine the usefulness of repetitive drill in basic skill areas with the power of interactivity offered by today's technology. Implement the latest appropriate technologies and approaches as they become available and appear feasible and effective in order to avail yourself and your students of more powerful and more musical applications of technology.

Technological tips

The following tips are drawn from the research that has been described in this book and represent some ideas that might prove to be practical for immediate classroom use. Readers are encouraged to use these tips as a beginning and a guide for the integration of technology into their teaching.

Computer-assisted instruction: General guidelines

- Use drill-and-practice software for reinforcing basic skills such as note naming and ear training.
- Do not expect drill-and-practice software to teach concepts.
- Tutorial software can be used for supplementary instruction on specific problem areas.

- Simulations can provide excellent settings for problem-solving strategies. Unfortunately, little simulation software has been developed specific to music education.
- When using an instructional game, make sure that it is instructional and not an empty activity.
- Teachers must provide the lesson structure when using computerized application programs. Application software does not teach, but teachers can use it to teach.

Musical skills

- Sequencers are very effective tools for teaching composition since they allow for easy manipulation of sound. Students can hear and then revise their compositions.
- Use CAI drill-and-practice programs to speed the process of learning to read musical notation.
- Individualize ear-training routines by "prescribing" the software and other technologies appropriate to each student's needs.
- Jump over traditional hurdles of music reading and performance skills by choosing notation software that accepts MIDI input.

Creativity

- Liberate the creative process by using gesture-based technologies for musical input.

Multimedia and hypermedia

- Multimedia is a tool for teaching, but teachers must provide the instructional framework for learning to take place.
- Hypermedia programs are intended for individual student use.
- Explore the potential of video for observing and practicing conducting and other performance skills.
- Hypermedia tutorials allow easy and unique manipulation of mixed media and hold great potential for music education.
- With CD-ROM tutorials, provide clear objectives to the learner so that his or her exploration of the materials can be focused.
- Help students develop appropriate learning strategies for dealing with the unique presentation of hypermedia tutorials.

Emerging technologies

- Currently available artificial intelligence systems are most valuable in domains that are rule based, such as music theory. Avail yourself of this new approach.

New ideas about teaching

- Most technology has a very narrowly defined purpose. Make sure that your instructional goals are realistic within the limitations of the particular technology.
- Integrate technology into your curriculum by correlating CAI programs with your instrumental method books.
- Make technical practice enjoyable with MIDI "Music Minus One." Sequence interesting accompaniments for scales and other technical exercises.
- In instrumental music classes, CAI can be used for individuals who forgot their instrument or who need extra help on certain areas.
- Use commercially available technologies to motivate; turn their popular appeal and novelty into educational advantage.
- Bridge the gap between "real" music and "school" music by integrating electronic keyboards into the traditional music curriculum.
- Integrate MIDI concepts into traditional piano classes by using new keyboard lab systems.
- Think of synthesizers not as machines but as *musical instruments* with their own unique performance techniques and requirements.
- Combine "older" proven technologies with newer technologies for increased learning achievement.
- To optimize the educational power of the computer, use computers in the classroom as regular teaching tools. Place computers in the classroom itself to promote and facilitate effective instructional use.

Summary

Instructional technology seems especially promising for music education because it allows the teacher to manipulate sound in unique ways that can be valuable in presenting information. In addition, the ability to easily manipulate sound allows students to study composition in more meaningful ways, since they are able to hear their work without the limitations inherent in live, acoustic performances.

Technology also allows new instructional models and methods to be employed. Some traditional practices can be improved upon, most notably the ability to drill students on discrete factual information by using drill-and-practice computer software; the computer can provide endless practice examples in a nonthreatening environment. Computers can also be used to provide individualized instruction, allowing the teacher greater freedom. With these tools, creative teachers can develop new and powerful teaching approaches.

Musical and educational technologies are new teaching tools to be used by teachers in ways to improve instruction. However, these new tools certainly do not automatically guarantee success. Technology will be of value only when it is used appropriately, in conjunction with sound teaching methods that are rooted in a good philosophical base. When thoughtfully integrated into music instruction by a musician-educator, these tools have potential to transform the music classroom.

References

Adams, S. M. (1990). The development of a computer-based interactive multimedia program for teaching interpretive aspects of wind instrument notation (Doctoral dissertation, University of Southern California, 1989). *Dissertation Abstracts International, 50,* 1841A.

Alessi, S. M., & Trollip, S. R. (1985). *Computer-based instruction.* Englewood Cliffs, NJ: Prentice-Hall.

Alessi, S. M., & Trollip, S. R. (1991). *Computer-based instruction* (2nd ed.). Englewood Cliffs, NJ: Prentice-Hall.

Alexander, P., & Judy, J. (1988). The interaction of domain-specific knowledge and strategic knowledge in academic performance. *Review of Educational Research, 58,* 375-404.

Allvin, R. L. (1970). Do colleges and universities need an automated music learning center? *Bulletin of the Council for Research in Music Education,* no. 21, 32-45.

Ambrose, D. W. (1991). The effects of hypermedia on learning: A literature review. *Educational Technology, 31* (12), 51-55.

Anderson, D. R., & Field, D. (1983). Children's attention to television: Implications for production. In M. Meyer (Ed.), *Children and the formal features of television* (pp. 56-96). Munich, Germany: Saur.

Apfelstadt, M. (1992). I want to use computers NOW (but we have no money). *Music Educators Journal, 79* (4), 12-14.

Appell, C. J. (1993). Keyboard instruction in the classroom. *Music Educators Journal, 79* (9), 21-24.

Arenson, M. (1979). Computer-based ear training instruction for non-music majors. In *Mission of the Future: Proceedings of the*

Annual Convention of the Association for the Development of Computer-Based Instructional Systems (pp. 949–958). (ERIC Document Reproduction Service No. ED 175 449)

Ashley, W., Konopka, E., & Carrico, L. R. (1983). *Preparing for high technology: Robotics programs.* Columbus, OH: Ohio State University, National Center for Research in Vocational Education. (ERIC Document Reproduction Service No. ED 228 472)

Atwater, D. F. (1992). The development and trial of computer-based interactive videodisc courseware for teaching skills in the visual diagnosis of selected problems in trombone performance (Doctoral dissertation, University of Illinois at Urbana-Champaign, 1991). *Dissertation Abstracts International, 52,* 2452A. (University Microfilms No. 9136532)

Baddeley, A. (1990). *Human memory: Theory and practice.* Boston: Allyn and Bacon.

Bailey, D. L. (1990). The effects of computer-based instruction on achievement of four-, five-, and six-year-old children in the Yamaha Music Education System Primary One Course (Doctoral dissertation, University of Illinois at Urbana-Champaign, 1989). *Dissertation Abstracts International, 51,* 777A.

Banks, D. W. (1990). The correlation of selected precollege music computer programs with the Alfred Basic Piano Library (Doctoral dissertation, University of Oklahoma, 1990). *Dissertation Abstracts International, 51,* 1819A.

Barden, R. (1989). Developing a HyperCard-based intelligent training system. *Educational and Training Technology International, 26,* 361–367.

Bare, A. C. (1988). The Organization Doctor: An expert tutor. *Collegiate Microcomputer, 6,* 317–323.

Barr, A., & Feigenbaum, E. A. (Eds.). (1986). *The handbook of artificial intelligence: Vol. II.* Reading, MA: Addison-Wesley.

Beasley, R. E. (1992). A methodology for collecting navigation data using IBM's Linkway: A hypermedia authoring language. *Journal of Educational Multimedia and Hypermedia, 1,* 465–470.

Beasley, R. E., & Vila, J. A. (1992). The identification of navigation patterns in a multimedia environment: A case study. *Journal of Educational Multimedia and Hypermedia, 1,* 209–222.

Berz, W. L. (1991). Hypertext and hypermedia: Computer interactive instruction in music. *1991 Proceedings of the Eleventh Annual Symposium on Small Computers in the Arts, 11,* 42–45.

Berz, W. L. (1991/1992, Fall/Winter). A hypermedia application using the University of Delaware Videodisc Music Series. *MusDisc News, 4* (1&2), 4–5.

Bowman, J. A. (1984). An investigation of two methods of preparation for college level music theory (Doctoral dissertation, University of Rochester, Eastman School of Music, 1984). *Dissertation Abstracts International, 45,* 779A.

Bowman, J. A. (1986). Contemporary techniques for contemporary students: Computer applications for prospective music teachers. [Abstract]. In *Association for the Development of Computer-Based Instructional Systems Conference Proceedings* (p. 442). Billingham, WA: Association for the Development of Computer-Based Instructional Systems. (ERIC Document Reproduction Service No. ED 278 378)

Bowers, D., & Tsai, C. (1990). HyperCard in educational research: An introduction and case study. *Educational Technology, 30* (2), 19–24.

Bresler, L. (1988). The role of the computer in a music theory classroom: Integration, barriers, and learning (Doctoral dissertation, Stanford University, 1987). *Dissertation Abstracts International, 48,* 1689A.

Brick, J. S. (1985). The importance of technology to aural/oral perception. *Update: Applications of Research in Music Education, 3* (3), 13–16.

Brotz, T. W. (1990). Key-finding, fingering, and timing tasks in entry-level piano performance of children (Doctoral dissertation, University of Kentucky, 1990). *Dissertation Abstracts International, 51,* 1150A.

Brown, J. S. (1990). Toward a new epistemology for learning. In C. Frasson & G. Gauthier (Eds.), *Intelligent tutoring systems: At the crossroad of artificial intelligence and education* (pp. 266–282). Norwood, NJ: Ablex Publishing.

Buck, B. (1991). An experimental study using the Pitch Master and TAP Master systems to improve music literacy and singing skills (Doctoral dissertation, Catholic University of America, 1991). *Dissertation Abstracts International, 52,* 2060A.

Burnett, A. J. (1991). An exploratory study of hypertext processing strategies (Doctoral dissertation, University of Pittsburgh, 1991). *Dissertation Abstracts International, 52,* 1717A.

Burns, H. L., & Capps, C. G. (1988). Foundations of intelligent tutoring systems: An introduction. In M. C. Polson & J. J. Richardson (Eds.), *Foundations of intelligent tutoring systems* (pp. 1–19). Hillsdale, NJ: Lawrence Erlbaum.

Bush, V. (1945, July). As we may think. *Atlantic Monthly,* pp. 101–108.

Callahan, G. L. (1986). The measurement of finger dexterity in woodwind and brass instrumentalists: A developmental study (Doctoral dissertation, Ohio State University, 1986). *Dissertation Abstracts International, 47,* 1641A.

Carlson, P. A. (1988). Hypertext: A way of incorporating user feedback into online documentation. In E. Barrett (Ed.), *Text, conText, and hyperText: Writing with and for the computer* (pp. 93-110). Cambridge, MA: MIT Press.

Chamberlin, L. L., Clark, R. W., & Svengalis, J. N. (1993). Success with keyboards in middle school. *Music Educators Journal, 79* (9), 31-35.

Chen, C. (1989). As we think: Thriving in the HyperWeb environment. *Microcomputers for Information Management, 6* (2), 77-97.

Clark, R. E. (1983). Reconsidering research on learning from media. *Review of Educational Research, 53,* 445-459.

Clark, R. E. (1985). Confounding in educational computing research. *Journal of Educational Computing Research, 1,* 137-148.

Coan, D. A. (1993). Computer-mediated communication for survey research in music education (Doctoral dissertation, University of Illinois at Urbana-Champaign, 1992). *Dissertation Abstracts International, 53,* 3467A.

Codding, P. A. (1986). The effect of differential feedback on beginning guitar students' intonational performance in tuning strings (Doctoral dissertation, Florida State University, 1985). *Dissertation Abstracts International, 46,* 2608A.

Colman, J. P. (1990). The development and validation of a computerized diagnostic test for the prediction of success in the first-year music theory sequence by incoming freshmen at Michigan State University (Doctoral dissertation, Michigan State University, 1990). *Dissertation Abstracts International, 51,* 1541A.

Conant, B. H. (1988). A study of cognitive processes of children creating music in a computer learning environment (Doctoral dissertation, University of Massachusetts, 1988). *Dissertation Abstracts International, 49,* 1086A.

Conklin, J. (1987). Hypertext: An introduction and survey. *IEEE Computer, 20* (9), 17-41.

Courtney, J. M. (1988). Computerized drill writing: A comparison of traditional marching band drill writing techniques with a computerized marching band drill writing package (Doctoral dissertation, Memphis State University, 1987). *Dissertation Abstracts International, 48,* 3005A.

Dalby, B. F. (1990). A computer-based training program for the development of harmonic intonation discrimination skill (Doctoral dissertation, University of Illinois at Urbana-

Champaign, 1989). *Dissertation Abstracts International, 50,* 1974A.

Dalby, B. F. (1992). A computer-based training program for developing harmonic intonation discrimination skill. *Journal of Research in Music Education, 40,* 139-152.

Dangelo, E. M. (1985). The use of computer based instruction in the teaching of music fundamentals (Doctoral dissertation, University of Pittsburgh, 1985). *Dissertation Abstracts International, 46,* 1550A.

Davidson, L. (1990). Tools and environments for musical creativity. *Music Educators Journal, 76* (9), 47-51.

Deal, J. J. (1984). Computer-assisted programmed instruction to teach pitch and rhythm error-detection skill to college music education students (Doctoral dissertation, University of Iowa, 1983). *Dissertation Abstracts International, 44,* 3622A.

Deal, J. J. (1985). Computer-assisted instruction in pitch and rhythm error detection. *Journal of Research in Music Education, 33,* 159-166.

Deihl, N. C. (1971). Computer-assisted instruction and instrumental music: Implications for teaching and research. *Journal of Research in Music Education, 19,* 299-306.

Deihl, N. C., & Radocy, R. E. (1969). Computer-assisted instruction: Potential for instrumental music education. *Bulletin of the Council for Research in Music Education,* no. 15, 1-7.

Dorin, W. J. (1990). The development of an expert system for developing instructional objectives (Doctoral dissertation, Purdue University, 1990). *Dissertation Abstracts International, 52,* 66A.

Draper, T. W., Cahoon, O. W., & Clayton, W. Y. (1986, March). *Making the computer fit the child rather than the child fit the computer: Conversations between children and robots.* Paper presented at the biennial meeting of the Southwestern Society for Research in Human Development, San Antonio, TX. (ERIC Document Reproduction Service No. ED 267 931)

Dunnigan, P. (1993). The computer in instrumental music. *Music Educators Journal, 80* (1), 32-37, 61.

Eddins, J. M. (1981). A brief history of computer-assisted instruction in music. *Journal of the College Music Symposium, 21* (2), 7-14.

Edmunds, R. A. (1988). *The Prentice Hall guide to expert systems.* Englewood Cliffs, NJ: Prentice Hall.

Eisele, M. J. (1986). Development and validation of a computer-assisted instructional lesson for teaching intonational discrimination skills to violin and viola students (Doctoral dissertation,

Indiana University, 1985). *Dissertation Abstracts International, 46,* 3642A.

Elieson, S. W. (1990). Development of an expert system to teach diagnostic skills (Doctoral dissertation, University of North Texas, 1990). *Dissertation Abstracts International, 51,* 2993A.

Etmektsoglou, I. E. (1993). A computer-based evaluation of pitch matching skills of college freshman students in music (Doctoral dissertation, University of Illinois at Urbana-Champaign, 1992). *Dissertation Abstracts International, 53,* 3836A.

Farmer, L. (1989). Hypertext: Links, nodes and associations. *Canadian Library Journal, 46,* 235-238.

Fisher, S. S. (1991). Virtual environments: Personal simulations & telepresence. In S. K. Helsel & J. P. Roth (Eds.), *Virtual reality* (pp. 101-110). London: Meckler.

Fleming, M. L. (1987a). Designing pictorial/verbal instruction: Some speculative extensions from research to practice. In D. M. Willows & H. A. Houghton (Eds.), *The psychology of illustration: Vol. 2. Instructional issues* (pp. 136-157). New York: Springer-Verlag.

Fleming, M. L. (1987b). Displays and communication. In R. M. Gagne (Ed.), *Instructional technology: Foundations* (pp. 233-260). Hillsdale, NJ: Lawrence Erlbaum.

Ford, L. (1987). Anatomy of an ICAI system. In R. Lewis & E. D. Tagg (Eds.), *Trends in computer assisted education* (pp. 22-31). Oxford: Blackwell Scientific Publications.

Forsythe, R. (1985). The development and implementation of a computerized preschool measure of musical audiation (Doctoral dissertation, Case Western Reserve University, 1984). *Dissertation Abstracts International, 45,* 2433A.

Fraase, M. (1990). *Macintosh hypermedia: Vol. II.* Glenview, IL: Scott, Foresman & Company.

Franklin, C. (1990). A bibliography on hypertext and hypermedia with selected annotations. *Database, 13* (1), 24-32.

Franklin, C., & Bessmer, L. (1990). A bibliography on hypertext continues...HyperCard stacks and tutorials. *Database, 13* (2), 38-45.

Frenzel, L. E., Jr. (1987). *Crash course in artificial intelligence and expert systems.* Indianapolis, IN: Howard W. Sams & Co.

Frey, D. K. (1989). A hypermedia lesson about 1875-1885 costume: Cognitive style, perceptual modes, anxiety, attitude, and achievement (Doctoral dissertation, Iowa State University, 1989). *Dissertation Abstracts International, 50,* 2767A.

Fritz, M. (1991). The world of virtual reality. *Training, 28* (2), 45-50.

Fry, R. J. (1993). Development and trial of a computer-based interactive videodisc program in a course in fundamentals of conducting (Doctoral dissertation, University of Illinois at Urbana-Champaign, 1992). *Dissertation Abstracts International, 53,* 3837A.

Fujihara, H., Snell, J. R., & Boyle, C. D. (1992). Intelligent search in an educational hypertext environment. *Journal of Educational Multimedia and Hypermedia, 1,* 401-415.

Gagne, R. M., & Glaser, R. (1987). Foundations in learning research. In R. M. Gagne (Ed.), *Instructional technology: Foundations* (pp. 49-83). Hillsdale, NJ: Lawrence Erlbaum.

Garg, P. K. (1989). Information management in software engineering: A hypertext-based approach (Doctoral dissertation, University of Southern California, 1989). *Dissertation Abstracts International, 50,* 2021B.

Garoogian, A. (1984). *Robotics, 1960-1983: An annotated bibliography.* Brooklyn, NY: CompuBibs.

Garton, B. G. (1989). Working with Elthar: An intelligent music interface (Doctoral dissertation, Princeton University, 1988). *Dissertation Abstracts International, 50,* 2293A.

Garton, J. C. (1982). The efficacy of computer-based and tape-recorded assistance in second-semester freshman ear-training instruction (Doctoral dissertation, Louisiana State University and Agricultural and Mechanical College, 1981). *Dissertation Abstracts International, 42,* 4756A.

Gates, E. E. (1985). The effect of multi-image, multi-media related arts programs on cognitive and affective learning by undergraduate non-music majors in a music literature course (Doctoral dissertation, University of Maryland at College Park, 1984). *Dissertation Abstracts International, 46,* 641A.

Gill, M. J. (1989). Zyklus: A performer's analysis: A videotaped timpani method utilizing computer assisted instruction for ear training (Doctoral dissertation, University of Southern Mississippi, 1988). *Dissertation Abstracts International, 50,* 16A.

Glass, J. S. (1986). The effects of a microcomputer-assisted tuning program on junior high school students' pitch discrimination and pitch-matching abilities (Doctoral dissertation, University of Miami, 1986). *Dissertation Abstracts International, 47,* 2070A.

Goodson, C. A. (1993). Intelligent music listening: An interactive hypermedia program for basic music listening skills (Doctoral dissertation, University of Utah, 1992). *Dissertation Abstracts*

International, 53, 3837A.

Goodwin, M. A. (1991). The effectiveness of "Pitch Master" compared to traditional classroom methods in teaching sightsinging to college music students (Doctoral dissertation, University of South Florida, 1990). *Dissertation Abstracts International, 52,* 106A.

Gray, R. A. (1988). Robots: A high-tech tool for the learner. *Techtrends, 33* (5), 45–48.

Haas, C. (1989). "Seeing it on the screen isn't really seeing it:" Computer writers' reading problems. In G. Hawisher & C. Selfe (Eds.), *Critical perspectives on computers and composition instruction* (pp. 16–29). New York: Teachers College Press.

Hall, W., Thorogood, P., Hutchings, G., & Carr, L. (1989). Using HyperCard and interactive video in education: An application in cell biology. *Educational & Training Technology International, 26,* 207–214.

Hamilton, J. H., III. (1989). A video assisted instructional program for bass drum and selected accessory percussion instruments (drum) (Doctoral dissertation, University of Southern Mississippi, 1988). *Dissertation Abstracts International, 50,* 113A.

Harris, C. R., & Brinkman, A. R. (1989). An integrated software system for set-theoretic and serial analysis of contemporary music. *Journal of Computer-Based Instruction, 16,* 59–70.

Heritage, R. A. (1986). A study of the effect of selected environmental and instructional factors on the aural skill achievement of college music majors (Doctoral dissertation, University of Southern Mississippi, 1986). *Dissertation Abstracts International, 47,* 4012A.

Hesser, L. A. (1988). Effectiveness of computer-assisted instruction in developing music reading skills at the elementary level (Doctoral dissertation, State University of New York at Albany, 1988). *Dissertation Abstracts International, 49,* 419A.

Higgins, W. R. (1981). The feasibility of teaching beginning applied clarinet with the microcomputer (Doctoral dissertation, Pennsylvania State University, 1981). *Dissertation Abstracts International, 42,* 126A.

Higgins, W. R. (1992). The development and validation of a microcomputer flute simulator for the purpose of computer-assisted instruction in flute. *Pennsylvania Music Educators Association: Bulletin of Research in Music Education, 18,* 36–43.

Hiranpradist, B. R. (1987). Formal operational thought as a dimension of music listener behavior (Doctoral dissertation, Michigan State University, 1986). *Dissertation Abstracts*

International, 47, 2362A.

Hirsch, L. S., Kelly, A. E., & O'Donnell, A. (1992). *Improving understanding of measurement and testing through the use of computer-based instruction.* Paper presented at the annual meeting of the Eastern Educational Research Association, Hilton Head, South Carolina.

Ho, T. K-L. (1991). The development of a computer-assisted approach to the teaching of violin tone production (Doctoral dissertation, Columbia University, Teachers College, 1990). *Dissertation Abstracts International, 51,* 2306A.

Hofstetter, F. T. (1975). GUIDO: An interactive computer-based system for improvement of instruction and research in ear-training. *Journal of Computer-Based Instruction, 1,* 40-42.

Hofstetter, F. T. (1977). Interactive simulation/games as an aid to musical learning. In *Proceedings of the 1977 Winter Conference of the Association for the Development of Computer-Based Instructional Systems* (pp. 104-117). Bellingham, WA: Association for the Development of Computer-Based Instructional Systems.

Hofstetter, F. T. (1978). Computer-based recognition of perceptual patterns in harmonic dictation exercises. *Journal of Research in Music Education, 26,* 111-119.

Hofstetter, F. T. (1979). Evaluation of a competency-based approach to teaching aural interval identification. *Journal of Research in Music Education, 27,* 210-213.

Hofstetter, F. T. (1980). Computer-based recognition of perceptual patterns in chordal quality dictation exercises. *Journal of Research in Music Education, 28,* 83-91.

Hofstetter, F. T. (1981a). Applications of the GUIDO system to aural skills research, 1975-80. *Journal of the College Music Symposium, 21* (2), 46-53.

Hofstetter, F. T. (1981b, November). *Computer-based instruction: Roots, origins, applications, benefits, features, systems, trends, and issues.* Paper prepared for the International Sales Meeting of the Digital Equipment Corporation, Jacksonville, FL. (ERIC Document Reproduction Service No. ED 231 343)

Hofstetter, F. T. (1981c). Computer-based recognition of perceptual patterns and learning styles in rhythmic dictation exercises. *Journal of Research in Music Education, 29,* 265-277.

Hofstetter, F. T. (1985). Perspectives on a decade of computer-based instruction, 1974-1984. *Journal of Computer-Based Instruction, 12,* 1-7.

Holland, M. (1987). The effect of computer instruction on the vertical/horizontal music reading skills of the grand staff for students enrolled in senior high school beginning keyboard classes

(Doctoral dissertation, University of South Carolina, 1987). *Dissertation Abstracts International, 48,* 862A.

Holland, S. (1986). *How computers are used in the teaching of music and speculations about how artificial intelligence could be applied to radically improve the learning of compositional skills.* Walton, Bletchley, Bucks (England): Open University, Institute of Educational Technology. (ERIC Document Reproduction Service No. ED 328 480)

Holland, S. (1989). Artificial intelligence, education and music: The use of artificial intelligence to encourage and facilitate music composition by novices. *Dissertation Abstracts International, 51,* 4054A. (ERIC Document Reproduction Service No. ED 329 452)

Holton, A. M., Jr. (1991). A study of children's preference for acoustical and synthesized timbre (Doctoral dissertation, Columbia University Teachers College, 1990). *Dissertation Abstracts International, 51,* 2307A.

Horney, M. (1993). A measure of hypertext linearity. *Journal of Educational Multimedia and Hypermedia, 2,* 67-82.

Hsieh, C. C., & Hall, W. (1989). Survey of artificial intelligence and expert systems in library and information science literature. *Information Technology and Libraries, 8,* 209-214.

Hughes, T. E. (1991). A hypermedia listening station for the college music literature class (Doctoral dissertation, University of Arizona, 1991). *Dissertation Abstracts International, 52,* 838A. (University Microfilms No. 9124153)

Hullfish, W. R. (1972). A comparison of two computer-assisted instructional programs in music theory. *Journal of Research in Music Education, 20,* 354-361.

Hultberg, M. L., Hultberg, W. E., & Tenny, T. (1979). Project CLEF: CAI in music theory. In *Mission of the Future: Proceedings of the Annual Convention of the Association for the Development of Computer-Based Instructional Systems* (pp. 928-934). Bellingham, WA: Association for the Development of Computer-Based Instructional Systems. (ERIC Document Reproduction Service No. ED 175 449)

Ingraham, B., & Emery, C. (1991). France InterActive: A hypermedia approach to language training. *Educational and Training Technology International, 28,* 321-333.

Irish, P. M., & Trigg, R. H. (1989). Supporting collaboration in hypermedia: Issues and experiences. *Journal of the American Society for Information Science, 40,* 192-199.

Isaak, T. J. (1989). The effectiveness of computerized drill and practice and bisensory input in teaching music-reading skills to elementary students (Doctoral dissertation, University of Northern Colorado, 1988). *Dissertation Abstracts International, 49,* 2185A.

Isler-Hamilton, E. J. (1990). The effect of instructional method on handicapped students' comprehension of specific music concepts: Computer versus noncomputer instruction (Doctoral dissertation, State University of New York at Buffalo, 1989). *Dissertation Abstracts International, 50,* 3204A.

Jacobsen, J. R. (1987). Effectiveness of a computer-assisted instruction program in music fundamentals applied to instruction for elementary education majors (Doctoral dissertation, University of Northern Colorado, 1986). *Dissertation Abstracts International, 47,* 3350A.

Jacobson, L. (1991). Virtual reality: A status report. *AI Expert, 6* (8), 26–33.

Jacobson, R. L. (1989). An expert system shell used to develop a knowledge-based information system to advise students (Doctoral dissertation, Wayne State University, 1989). *Dissertation Abstracts International, 51,* 728A.

Jonassen, D. H. (1988). Designing structured hypertext and structuring access to hypertext. *Educational Technology, 28* (11), 13–16.

Jonassen, D. H. (1991). Hypertext as instructional design. *Educational Technology Research and Development, 39* (1), 83–92.

Jonassen, D. H. (1992). Editorial: Learning vs. information. *Journal of Educational Multimedia and Hypermedia, 1,* 3–5.

Jonassen, D. H., & Wang, S. (1993). Acquiring structural knowledge from semantically structured hypertext. *Journal of Computer-Based Instruction, 20,* 1–8.

Jones, D. L. (1991). Design and trial of a computer-based system supplying practice in error detection for preservice instrumental music educators (Doctoral dissertation, University of Georgia, 1990). *Dissertation Abstracts International, 51,* 3355A.

Jones, J. A., Miller, B. O., & Scarborough, D. L. (1988). A rule-based expert system for music perception. *Behavior Research Methods, Instruments, & Computers, 20,* 255–262.

Kassner, K. (1993). Effects of computer-assisted instruction in a mastery learning/cooperative learning setting on the playing abilities and attitudes of beginning band students (Doctoral dissertation, University of Illinois at Urbana-Champaign, 1992). *Dissertation Abstracts International, 53,* 2728A.

Kearsley, G. (1988). Authoring considerations for hypertext. *Educational Technology, 28* (11), 21–24.

Keramas, J. G. (1990). Curriculum development of robotics/automated systems for vocational education at the secondary level based on an industry needs assessment (Doctoral dissertation, University of Massachusetts, 1990). *Dissertation Abstracts International, 51,* 3619A.

King, R. V. (1989). The effects of computer-assisted music instruction on achievement of seventh-grade students (Doctoral dissertation, University of Illinois at Urbana-Champaign, 1988). *Dissertation Abstracts International, 49,* 2574A.

Kinzie, M. B., & Berdel, R. L. (1990). Design and use of hypermedia systems. *Educational Technology Research and Development, 38* (3), 61–68.

Kissinger, P. (1987). Artificial intelligence, robots and education: Selected sources. *Education Libraries, 12* (3), 81–84.

Klappenberger, F. A. (1990). The effect of domain knowledge on searching for specific information in a hypertext environment (Doctoral dissertation, University of Maryland at College Park, 1990). *Dissertation Abstracts International, 51,* 3620A.

Knox-Quinn, C. (1988). A simple application and a powerful idea: Using expert system shells in the classroom. *The Computing Teacher, 16* (2), 12–15.

Knox-Quinn, C. H. (1991). Student construction of expert systems: Impact on content area learning and problem-solving (Doctoral dissertation, University of Oregon, 1991). *Dissertation Abstracts International, 52,* 1298A.

Knuth, R. A. (1993). Hypermedia and learning: The case of intermedia (Doctoral dissertation, Indiana University, 1992). *Dissertation Abstracts International, 53,* 3879A.

Kolb, R. M. (1985). A real-time microcomputer-assisted system for translating aural, monophonic tones into music notation as an aid to sightsinging (Doctoral dissertation, Louisiana State University and Agricultural and Mechanical College, 1984). *Dissertation Abstracts International, 45,* 2297A.

Konecky, L. W. (1987). A comparison of two sequences of aural interval identification drill administered to college students through computer-assisted instruction (Doctoral dissertation, University of Southern Mississippi, 1986). *Dissertation Abstracts International, 47,* 4013A.

Kozerski, R. A. (1989). Personal computer microworlds for music composition and education (Doctoral dissertation, University of California, San Diego, 1988). *Dissertation Abstracts International, 50,* 17A.

Kozma, R. B. (1991). Learning with media. *Review of Educational*

Research, 61, 179-211.

Krondracke, M. (1992). The official word: How our government views the use of computers in schools. *Macworld, 9* (9), 232-236.

Krueger, M. W. (1991a). *Artificial reality II.* Reading, MA: Addison-Wesley.

Krueger, M. W. (1991b). Artificial reality: Past and future. In S. K. Helsel & J. P. Roth (Eds.), *Virtual reality* (pp. 19-25). London: Meckler.

Kuhn, W. E. (1974). Computer-assisted instruction in music: Drill and practice in dictation. *Journal of the College Music Symposium, 14,* 89-101.

Kuhn, W. E., & Allvin, R. L. (1967). Computer-assisted teaching: A new approach to research in music. *Journal of Research in Music Education, 15,* 305-315.

Kulik, J. A., Bangert-Downs, R. L., & Williams, G. W. (1983). Effects of computer-based teaching on secondary school students. *Journal of Educational Psychology, 75,* 19-26.

Kulik, C. C., Kulik, J. A., & Bangert-Downs, R. L. (1984, April). *Effects of computer-based education on elementary school pupils.* A symposium paper presented at the annual meeting of the American Educational Research Association, New Orleans.

Kulik, J. A., & Kulik, C. L. (1987, February). *Computer-based instruction: What 200 evaluations say.* Paper presented at the annual convention of the Association of Educational Communications and Technology, Atlanta, GA. (ERIC Document Reproduction Service No. ED 285 521)

Kulik, J. A., Kulik, C. C., & Bangert-Downs, R. L. (1985). The importance of outcome studies: A reply to Clark. *Journal of Educational Computing Research, 1,* 381-387.

Kulik, J. A., Kulik, C. C., & Cohen, P. A. (1980). Effectiveness of computer-based college teaching: A meta-analysis of findings. *Review of Educational Research, 50,* 525-544.

Kuyper, J. Q. (1982). MISTI: A computer-assisted instruction system in music theory and fundamentals (Doctoral dissertation, University of Iowa, 1981). *Dissertation Abstracts International, 42,* 4641A.

Lanza, A., & Roselli, R. (1991). Effects of the hypertextual approach versus the structured approach on students' achievement. *Journal of Computer-Based Instruction, 18,* 48-50.

Leblanc, P. J. (1990). The development of computer-aided composition software and its implications for composition (Doctoral dissertation, University of Massachusetts, 1990). *Dissertation*

Abstracts International, 51, 771A.

Lee, Y. B. (1989). Effects of learning style and instructional cues on achievement and learning interactivity in a hypermedia instructional system (Doctoral dissertation, Purdue University, 1989). *Dissertation Abstracts International, 51,* 484A.

Lefrere, P., Waller, R. H. W., & Whalley, P. (1987). 'Expert systems' in educational technology? In N. Rushby (Ed.), *Technology based learning: Selected readings* (pp. 175–180). London: Kogan Page.

Legree, P. J., & Gillis, P. D. (1991). Product effectiveness evaluation criteria for intelligent tutoring systems. *Journal of Computer-Based Instruction, 18,* 57–62.

Lemons, R. M. (1985). The development and trial of microcomputer-assisted techniques to supplement traditional training in musical sightreading (Doctoral dissertation, University of Colorado at Boulder, 1984). *Dissertation Abstracts International, 45,* 2023A.

Leppla, D. A. (1990). The acquisition of basic conducting skills by beginning conductors: A comparison of the effects of guided and unguided videotaped modeling (Doctoral dissertation, Ohio State University, 1989). *Dissertation Abstracts International, 50,* 3509A.

Levie, W. H. (1987). Research on pictures: A guide to the literature. In D. M. Willows & H. A. Houghton (Eds.), *The psychology of illustration: Vol. 1. Basic research* (pp. 1–50). New York: Springer-Verlag.

Lin, X. (1988). A selected hypertext bibliography. *Educational Technology, 28* (11), 41–42.

Locatis, C., Letoumeau, G., & Banvard, R. (1989). Hypermedia and instruction. *Educational Technology Research and Development, 37* (4), 65–77.

Lomax, E. L. (1991). A comparison of three approaches to teach note-reading and note location on the piano keyboard to children, ages four to six (Doctoral dissertation, University of Missouri, Kansas City, 1990). *Dissertation Abstracts International, 51,* 2307A.

Lorek, M. J. (1991). Algorithms and criteria for a computer simulation of the evaluation of student sight singing ability by college music faculty (Doctoral dissertation, Florida State University, 1990). *Dissertation Abstracts International, 51,* 2307A.

Malave, J. E. (1991). A computer-assisted aural-visual approach to improve beginning students' clarinet tone (Doctoral dissertation, University of Texas at Austin, 1990). *Dissertation Abstracts International, 51,* 3355A.

Marchionini, G., & Shneiderman, B. (1988). Finding facts vs. browsing knowledge in hypertext systems. *IEEE Computer, 21,* 70–80.

Martindale, E. S. (1987). An expert system to train secondary special education teachers in language arts instruction (Doctoral dissertation, Utah State University, 1987). *Dissertation Abstracts International, 49,* 2627A.

Mayson, W. A., Jr. (1982). Organizing the instrumental music ensemble library with the aid of a machine-assisted system (Doctoral dissertation, Ohio State University, 1982). *Dissertation Abstracts International, 43,* 13A.

Maxwell, H. J., Jr. (1985). An artificial intelligence approach to computer-implemented analysis of harmony in tonal music (Doctoral dissertation, Indiana University, 1984). *Dissertation Abstracts International, 46,* 14A.

McArthur, V. H. (1992). Are computers doing their job? The effectiveness and attitudes surrounding micro-computer instructional use in the private music studio. *The Quarterly Journal of Music Teaching and Learning, 3* (2), 24–30.

McCloy, D., & Harris, D. M. J. (1986). *Robotics: An introduction.* New York: Halsted Press.

McConnell, B. A., & McConnell, N. J. (1988). A starter's guide to artificial intelligence. *Collegiate Microcomputer, 6,* 239–246.

McEneaney, J. E. (1991). A prototype expert system with applications in teacher training and the diagnosis remediation of reading problems. *Computers in the Schools, 8,* 315-317.

McGreer, D. M. (1984). The research literature in computer-assisted instruction. *Update: Applications of Research in Music Education, 3* (1), 12–15.

McNeil, B., & Nelson, K. R. (1991). Meta-analysis of interactive video instruction: A 10-year review of achievement effects. *Journal of Computer-Based Instruction, 18,* 1–6.

Meckley, W. A. (1985). The development of individualized music learning sequences for non-handicapped, handicapped and gifted learners using the LOGO Music Version computer language (Doctoral dissertation, University of Rochester, Eastman School of Music, 1985). *Dissertation Abstracts International, 45,* 190A.

Mee, R. A. (1989). The integration of "MusicLand" in a music listening course and acoustics course for tenth grade students (Doctoral dissertation, University of Rochester, Eastman School of Music, 1988). *Dissertation Abstracts International, 49,* 1727A.

Meehan, J. R. (1979). *An artificial intelligence approach to tonal music theory* (Tech. Rep. No. 124A). Irvine, CA: University of

California, Department of Information and Computer Services.

Mende, D. (1993). Telecommunications. *Tempo, 47* (4), 38-39.

Midoro, V., Olimpo, G., Persico, D., & Sarti, L. (1991). Multimedia navigable systems and artificial intelligence. In R. Lewis & S. Otsuki (Eds.), *Advanced research on computers in education* (pp. 179-184). North-Holland, The Netherlands: Elsevier Science Publishers B. V.

Miller, A. W. (1988). Feasibility of instruction in instrumental music education with an interactive videodisc adapted from existing media (Doctoral dissertation, University of Illinois at Urbana-Champaign, 1987). *Dissertation Abstracts International, 48,* 143A.

Miller, G. A. (1956). The magical number seven, plus or minus two: Some limits on our capacity for processing information. *Psychological Review, 63,* 81-97.

Misanchuk, E. R., & Schwier, R. A. (1992). Representing interactive multimedia and hypermedia audit trails. *Journal of Educational Multimedia and Hypermedia, 1,* 355-372.

Moore, B. R. (1991). *Music in education: Review of research.* Grand Rapids, MI: Yamaha Corporation of America.

Nash, M. (1989). *Computers, automation, and cybernetics.* Wilmington, DE: Hagley Museum and Library.

Nelson, A. C. (1990). Jester software and user manual (Original Computer Program). (Master's thesis, San Jose State University, 1989). *Masters Abstracts International, 28,* 474.

Nelson, B. J. P. (1989). The development of a middle school general music curriculum: A synthesis of computer-assisted instruction and music learning theory (Doctoral dissertation, University of Rochester, Eastman School of Music, 1988). *Dissertation Abstracts International, 49,* 1728A.

Nelson, B. J. P. (1991). The development of a middle school general music curriculum: A synthesis of computer-assisted instruction and music learning theory. *Southeastern Journal of Music Education, 3,* 141-148.

Nelson, W. A., & Palumbo, D. B. (1992). Learning, instruction, and hypermedia. *Journal of Educational Multimedia and Hypermedia, 1,* 287-299.

Newquist, H. P., III. (1991). A computer-generated suspension of disbelief. *AI Expert, 6* (8), 34-39.

Niemiec, R. P., Sikorski, M. F., & Walberg, H. J. (1989). Comparing the cost-effectiveness of tutoring and computer-based instruction. *Journal of Educational Computing Research, 5,* 395-407.

Ortner, J. M. (1991). The effectiveness of a computer-assisted instruction program in rhythm for secondary school instrumental music students (Doctoral dissertation, State University of New York at Buffalo, 1990). *Dissertation Abstracts International, 52,* 1249A.

Ozeas, N. L. (1991). The effect of the use of a computer assisted drill program on the aural skill development of students in beginning solfège (Doctoral dissertation, University of Pittsburgh, 1991). *Dissertation Abstracts International, 52,* 3553A.

Palitawanont, N. (1989). An investigation into the effectiveness of intelligent tutoring on learning of college level statistics (Doctoral dissertation, University of North Texas, 1989). *Dissertation Abstracts International, 50,* 1636A.

Pantelidis, V. S. (1991). *Robotics in education: An information guide.* Metuchen, NJ: Scarecrow Press.

Parker, R. C. (1980). The relative effectiveness of the TAP system in instruction in sight singing: An experimental study (Doctoral dissertation, University of Miami, 1979). *Dissertation Abstracts International, 41,* 151A.

Pawson, R. (1988). What is the role of the personal robot? In C. Terry & P. Thomas (Eds.), *Teaching & learning with robots* (pp. 1-8). London: Croom Helm.

Pembrook, R. G. (1986). Some implications of students' attitudes toward a computer-based melodic dictation program. *Journal of Research in Music Education, 34,* 121-133.

Peters, G. D. (1974). Feasibility of computer-assisted instruction for instrumental music education (Doctoral dissertation, University of Illinois at Urbana-Champaign, 1974). *Dissertation Abstracts International, 35,* 1478-1479A.

Peters, G. D. (1979). Courseware development for microcomputer based education in music. In *Mission of the Future: Proceedings of the Annual Convention of the Association for the Development of Computer-Based Instructional Systems* (pp. 922-927). Bellingham, WA: Association for the Development of Computer-Based Instructional Systems. (ERIC Document Reproduction Service No. ED 175 449)

Peters, G. D. (1981). Hardware development for computer-based instruction. *Journal of the College Music Symposium, 21* (2), 15-21.

Peters, G. D. (1992). *Musical skills: A computer-based assessment.* Urbana, IL: Council for Research in Music Education.

Placek, R. W. (1972). Design and trial of a computer-assisted lesson in rhythm (Doctoral dissertation, University of Illinois at Urbana-Champaign, 1972). *Dissertation Abstracts International,*

34, 320A.

Placek, R. W. (1974). Design and trial of a computer-assisted lesson in rhythm. *Journal of Research in Music Education, 22,* 13-23.

Platte, J. D. (1981). The effects of a microcomputer-assisted instructional program on the ability of college choral ensemble members to sing melodic configurations at sight (Doctoral dissertation, Ball State University, 1981). *Dissertation Abstracts International, 42,* 1360A.

Post, P. E., Howell, R. D., & Rakocy, L. (1988). Robot technology: Implications for education. *Educational Technology, 28* (1), 39-45.

Rada, R. (1989). Writing and reading hypertext: An overview. *Journal of the American Society for Information Science, 40* (3), 164-171.

Rada, R., & Murphy, C. (1992). Searching versus browsing in hypertext. *Hypermedia, 4,* 1-30.

Renfrow, K. D. (1991). The development and evaluation of objectives for educating graduate piano pedagogy students to use computer and keyboard technology (computer technology) (Doctoral dissertation, University of Oklahoma, 1991). *Dissertation Abstracts International, 52,* 2063A.

Robinson, R. L. (1984). The development and evaluation of a microcomputer-assisted music instruction program for the improvement of tonal memory (Doctoral dissertation, University of Miami, 1984). *Dissertation Abstracts International, 45,* 1065A.

Robinson, R. L. (1987). Uses of computers in music education: Past, present, and future. *Update: Application of Research in Music Technology, 5* (2), 12-15.

Rodriguez, E. S. (1992). The use of HyperCard in the development of software for creative elementary keyboard activities (Doctoral dissertation, Columbia University, Teachers College, 1991). *Dissertation Abstracts International, 52,* 3854A.

Rosenberg, R. (1987). A critical analysis of research on intelligent tutoring systems. *Educational Technology, 27* (11), 7-13.

Salame, P., & Baddeley, A. (1989). Effects of background music on phonological short-term memory. *The Quarterly Journal of Experimental Psychology, 41A,* 107-122.

Sanders, W. H. (1980). The effect of computer-based instructional materials in a program for visual diagnostic skills training of instrumental music education students (Doctoral dissertation, University of Illinois at Urbana-Champaign, 1980). *Dissertation Abstracts International, 41,* 2492A.

Schaffer, J. W. (1988a). Developing an intelligent music tutorial: An investigation of expert systems and their potential for microcomputer-based instruction in music theory (Doctoral dissertation, Indiana University, 1988). *Dissertation Abstracts International, 49,* 2959A.

Schaffer, J. W. (1988b). *Microcomputer-based intelligent tutoring systems: An assessment.* Unpublished manuscript, University of Wisconsin, Madison. (ERIC Document Reproduction Service No. ED 307 196)

Schaffer, J. W. (1991). Harmony Coach: An exploration of microcomputer-based intelligent tutoring systems in music. *Journal of Computer-Based Instruction, 18,* 30-36.

Schoeffler, C. F. (1990). A quasi-experimental study using Heathkit robots, EasyCAD and personal computers to teach robotics in the industrial technology curriculum in the high school grades (Master's thesis, University of Idaho, 1990). *Masters Abstracts International, 29,* 17.

Schopp, S. E. (1993). Electronic bulletin boards and the music educator. *Music Educators Journal, 79* (9), 64-66.

Schouten, J. F. (1989). The development and pilot testing of a knowledge structure for the systematic management of data about music, musicians, and music education (Doctoral dissertation, University of Illinois at Urbana-Champaign, 1988). *Dissertation Abstracts International, 50,* 382A.

Schultz, C. A. (1986, February). *A project in robotics education.* Paper presented at the Florida Instruction Computing Conference, Miami. (ERIC Document Reproduction Service No. ED 278 375)

Sener, E. M. (1991). Using microcomputers and an expert shell for soil conservation. *Collegiate Microcomputer, 9,* 7-12.

Shannon, D. W. (1982). Aural-visual interval recognition in music instruction: A comparison of a computer-assisted approach and a traditional in-class approach (Doctoral dissertation, University of Southern California, 1982). *Dissertation Abstracts International, 43,* 718A.

Shneiderman, B., Brethauer, D., Plaisant, C., & Potter, R. (1989). Evaluating three museum installations of a hypertext system. *Journal of the American Society for Information Science, 40* (3), 172-182.

Sigurjonsson, J. H. (1991). Interaction of college students with twentieth century music in a computer environment (Doctoral dissertation, University of Illinois at Urbana-Champaign, 1991). *Dissertation Abstracts International, 52,* 838A.

Simoni, M. H. (1983). The computer analysis of atonal music: An application program using set theory (Doctoral dissertation, Michigan State University, 1983). *Dissertation Abstracts*

International, 45, 14A.

Skelton, D. L. (1989). The implementation of a model program of computer-assisted instruction for children's choirs in a church setting (Doctoral dissertation, Southern Baptist Theological Seminary, 1988). *Dissertation Abstracts International, 50,* 382.

Small, R. V., & Grabowski, B. L. (1992). An exploratory study of information-seeking behaviors and learning with hypermedia information systems. *Journal of Educational Multimedia and Hypermedia, 1,* 445-464.

Sorisio, L. B. (1987, November). An Intelligent Tutoring System in Harmony [Abstract]. In *Association for the Development of Computer-Based Instructional Systems Conference Proceedings* (p. 371). Bellingham, WA: Association for the Development of Computer-Based Instructional Systems. (ERIC Document Reproduction Service No. ED 294 567)

Spring, M. B. (1991). Informating with virtual reality. In S. K. Helsel & J. P. Roth (Eds.), *Virtual reality* (pp. 3-17). London: Meckler.

Stanton, N. A., Taylor, R. G., & Tweedie, L. A. (1992). Maps as navigational aids in hypertext environments: An empirical evaluation. *Journal of Educational Multimedia and Hypermedia, 1,* 431-444.

Steinberg, E. R. (1992). The potential of computer-based telecommunications for instruction. *Journal of Computer-Based Instruction, 19,* 42-46.

Strange, C. M. (1991). The development of a beginning violin curriculum integrating a computer music station with the principles of comprehensive musicianship (Doctoral dissertation, Columbia University, Teachers College, 1990). *Dissertation Abstracts International, 51,* 2309A.

Stubbs, M., & Piddock, P. (1987). Artificial intelligence in teaching and learning: An introduction. In N. Rushby (Ed.), *Technology based learning: Selected readings* (pp. 166-174). London: Kogan Page.

Suppes, P., & Macken, E. (1978). The historical path from research and development to operational use of CAI. *Educational Technology, 18* (4), 9-12.

Syal, D. M. (1992). Computer implementation in music instruction: Grades K through 8. *Pennsylvania Music Educators Association: Bulletin of Research in Music Education, 18,* 65-76.

Tang, H., Barden, R., & Clifton, C. (1991). A new learning environment based on hypertext and ITS techniques. In R. Lewis & S. Otsuki (Eds.), *Advanced research on computers in education* (pp. 119-127). North-Holland, The Netherlands: Elsevier Science Publishers B. V.

Tennyson, R. D., & Park, O. C. (1987). Artificial intelligence and computer-based learning. In R. M. Gagne & R. Glaser (Eds.), *Instructional technology: Foundations* (pp. 319-342). Hillsdale, NJ: Lawrence Erlbaum.

Tidewater Technology Associates. (1990). Robotics: An emerging technology. *The Technology Teacher, 49* (5), 15-22.

Traub, D. C. (1991). Simulated world as classroom: The potential for designed learning with virtual environments. In S. K. Helsel & J. P. Roth (Eds.), *Virtual reality* (pp. 111-121). London: Meckler.

Tripp, S. D., & Roby, W. (1990). Orientation and disorientation in a hypertext lesson. *Journal of Computer-Based Instruction, 17* (4), 120-124.

Tsai, C. (1989). The effects of cognitive load of learning and prior achievement in the hypertext environment (Doctoral dissertation, Florida State University, 1989). *Dissertation Abstracts International, 50,* 670A.

Turk, G. C. (1985). Development of the music listening strategy TEMPO: Computer assisted instruction in music listening (Doctoral dissertation, University of Kansas, 1984). *Dissertation Abstracts International, 45,* 2436A.

Van Dam, A. (1988). Hypertext '87 keynote address. In *Hypertext on Hypertext* (HyperCard stack). New York: Association for Computing Machinery.

Van Scoyoc, M. L. (1992). The development and evaluation of electronic wind instrument controller instructional materials and techniques for the instrumental music educator (Doctoral dissertation, Columbia University, Teachers College, 1991). *Dissertation Abstracts International, 52,* 3213A.

Venn, M. L. (1991). An investigation of the applicability of recent advances in computer technology to the development of a computer-based, random-access audio test of common criterion-referenced objectives in elementary music (Doctoral dissertation, University of Illinois at Urbana-Champaign, 1990). *Dissertation Abstracts International, 51,* 309A.

Vispoel, W. P. (1993a). The development and evaluation of a computerized adaptive test of tonal memory. *Journal of Research in Music Education, 41,* 111-136.

Vispoel, W. P. (1993b). Recent research in computerized adaptive testing of musical aptitude. *Update: Applications of Research in Music Education, 11* (2), 39-41.

Vispoel, W. P., & Coffman, D. D. (1992). Computerized adaptive testing of music-related skills. *Bulletin of the Council of Research in*

Music Education, no. 112, 29–49.

Vitale, M. R., & Romance, N. R. (1991). Expert systems technology in teacher education: Applications and implications. *Computers in the Schools, 8,* 319–322.

Von Feldt, J. R. (1971). Computer-assisted instruction in the public school general music class: A comparative study (Doctoral dissertation, University of Missouri–Kansas City, 1971). *Dissertation Abstracts International, 33,* 2418A.

Wagner, S. P. (1991). Robotics and children: Their relationship to science achievement, problem-solving, ADHD rating scale scores, and learning styles (Doctoral dissertation, Florida Institute of Technology, 1991). *Dissertation Abstracts International, 52,* 1280A.

Watanabe, N. T. (1982). Computer-assisted music instruction: Utilizing compatible audio hardware in computer-assisted aural drill (Doctoral dissertation, University of Illinois at Urbana-Champaign, 1981). *Dissertation Abstracts International, 42,* 3900A.

Weeks, D. G. (1987). The effectiveness of using computer-assisted instruction with beginning trumpet students: Doctoral dissertation, Boston University. Reviewed by J. D. Secrest. In *Bulletin of the Council for Research in Music Education* (1989), no. 102, 89–94.

Whiston, S. K. (1987). The development of melodic concepts in elementary school age children using computer-assisted instruction as a supplemental tool (Doctoral dissertation, Ohio State University, 1986). *Dissertation Abstracts International, 47,* 3607A.

White, B. A. (1990). The development and implementation of an expert system for the advisement of undergraduate business administration majors (Doctoral dissertation, University of Nebraska-Lincoln, 1990). *Dissertation Abstracts International, 52,* 388A.

White, D. J. K. (1990). The discrimination and categorization of pitch direction by the young child (Doctoral dissertation, University of Washington, 1989). *Dissertation Abstracts International, 50,* 3790A.

Wiggins, J. (1993). Elementary music with synthesizers. *Music Educators Journal, 79* (9), 25–30.

Willett, B., & Netusil, A. (1989). Music computer drill and learning styles at the fourth-grade level. *Journal of Research in Music Education, 37,* 219–229.

Wilson, M. L. P. (1981). The development of CAI programs for teaching music fundamentals to undergraduate elementary education music methods classes (Doctoral dissertation, Louisiana State University and Agricultural and Mechanical College, 1981). *Dissertation Abstracts International, 42,* 1044A.

Winteregg, S. L. (1987). The future of the symphony orchestra based upon its historical development (Doctoral dissertation, Ohio State University, 1987). *Dissertation Abstracts International, 48,* 1053A.

Wixom, G. S. (1990). The development of an expert system for use in the evaluation of vocational training programs in Utah postsecondary institutions (Doctoral dissertation, Brigham Young University, 1990). *Dissertation Abstracts International, 51,* 2601A.

Woolf, B. (1988). Intelligent tutoring systems: A survey. In H. E. Shrobe & the American Association for Artificial Intelligence (Eds.), *Exploring artificial intelligence* (pp. 1-43). San Mateo, CA: Morgan Kaufmann Publisher.

Woolf, B. (1990). 20 years in the trenches: What have we learned? In C. Frasson & G. Gauthier (Eds.), *Intelligent tutoring systems: At the crossroad of artificial intelligence and education* (pp. 234-250). Norwood, NJ: Ablex Publishing.

Woolf, B. (1991). Representing, acquiring, and reasoning about tutoring knowledge. In R. Lewis & S. Otsuki (Eds.), *Advanced research on computers in education* (pp. 39-49). North-Holland, The Netherlands: Elsevier Science Publishers B. V.

Wright, J. C., Huston, A. C., Ross, R. P., Calvert, S. L., Tolandelli, D., Weeks, L. A., Raeissi, P., & Potts, R. (1984). Pace and continuity of television programs: Effects on children's attention and comprehension. *Developmental Psychology, 20,* 653-666.

Yazdani, M. (1986). Intelligent tutoring systems survey. *Artificial Intelligence Review, 1,* 43-52.

Yazdani, M. (1987). Intelligent tutoring systems: An overview. In R. W. Lawler & M. Yazdani (Eds.), *Artificial intelligence and education: Volume 1. Learning environments and tutoring systems* (pp. 183-201). Norwood, NJ: Ablex Publishing.

Glossary

Analog: A term referring to information that is not represented in numerical form.

Application software: A program that is designed to make some function easier to perform. The most common types of general application software include word processors, data bases, and spreadsheets; common applications in music include sequencers, music notation programs, and marching band drill writing software. Each type lets the user execute some function more easily than would be possible without it. This is sometimes referred to as tool software.

Artificial intelligence (AI): Those areas of computer science that attempt to duplicate certain functions performed by the human body and mind.

BASIC: A programming language that is fairly easy to learn and has been widely used with microcomputers (Beginners' All-purpose Symbolic Instruction Code).

Bit: The smallest unit of information recognized by a computer, a single character of 1 or 0.

Byte: A standard unit of measurement of computer information, usually a sequence of 8 binary units.

CAI: Computer-assisted instruction. This usually implies use of specialized computer software designed especially for teaching.

Card: (1) A board that is added to the inside of a computer to provide some added function, usually adding speed, memory, or the capability to perform some added ability such as digitizing. (2) What is seen on the computer screen in a HyperCard application.

CD-ROM: Compact disc–read only memory. A removable disk

with data that may be read but not modified. The disk may contain music or other data.

Courseware: A computer program or series of programs designed for teaching, often directed toward a single instructional goal. The program is usually accompanied by ancillary teaching materials.

DAC board: A specialized computer add-on that is placed inside of the computer to convert analog sounds to a digital format (analog to digital converter).

Digital: A term referring to information that is represented in numerical form.

Digitize: A process of converting analog information, such as music or video, into a set of numbers so that the information can be presented and processed by a computer.

Drill-and-practice software: A type of computer-assisted instruction program that provides practice material in a given subject under the assumption that the student is already familiar with the material to at least some degree. It is a set of electronic flash cards of sorts.

Expert system: Computer programs that use artificial intelligence techniques designed to mimic the performance of human experts in a given domain.

Field dependent: A cognitive style (way of approaching a learning task) in which people tend to accept a perceptual field as it is given, i.e., to accept learning material as it is presented. Such people prefer human interaction and do well in a teacher-organized lecture approach.

Field independent: A cognitive style (way of approaching a learning task) in which people tend to analyze and reorganize a perceptual field, i.e., to restructure learning material in their own way. Such people work well in self-directed discovery approaches and can profit from individualized learning approaches such as CAI.

Hardware: The physical parts of a computer system.

Hawthorne effect: A phenomenon in which some factors (subjects' awareness that they are participating in an experiment, novelty, special procedures used) may cause the participants in a study to perform in a way that is different from how they might perform under natural circumstances.

HyperCard: An object-oriented computer program developed by Apple Computers. It is used as a programming platform for many multimedia and hypermedia educational applications.

Hypermedia: An interactive multimedia application where the user can determine order of presentation and choice of media used for presentation.

Hypertalk: The scripting language used in HyperCard.

Hypertext: Nonlinear organization of text.

Instructional game software: A type of computer-assisted instruction program that is a modification of one of the other types of CAI, usually drill and practice or simulation, with the addition of a game component. Ideally, games provide greater motivation for students than "normal" CAI.

Intelligent tutoring system (ITS): An educational computer program that presents information based on the actions of the learner. The tutor "adapts" to meet the student's needs. It is an application of artificial intelligence.

Interface: (1) The electronic circuitry that allows different computers or parts of computers to be connected. (2) The relationship between the user and the machine.

Kilobyte (K): A unit of measure of the capacity of computer memory or storage space on a disc equivalent to 1,024 characters.

LOGO: A programming language developed for the purpose of teaching young children how to program.

Long-term memory (LTM): Many psychologists recognize two types of memory storage in humans: short-term memory and long-term memory. LTM is the main storage area for more lasting memories.

Mainframe: A large-scale, powerful computer.

Megabyte (MB): A unit of measure of the capacity of computer memory or storage space on a disc roughly equal to a million characters; also called a meg.

Meta-analysis: A technique of statistical analysis. A critical study of a large number of previous studies that provides an overview of a particular research area.

Microworld: A computer environment that actively engages students in creative activities, e.g., use of application (tool) software such as a notation program to teach composition.

MIDI: A communication protocol that allows communication between various musical instruments and/or computers (Musical Instrument Digital Interface).

Multimedia: A method of displaying any combination of text, sound (musical or otherwise), and/or pictures (still, animation, or video) into a presentation.

Pitch Master: A learning station centering on pitch developed by

Temporal Acuity Products.

RAM: Random-access memory, reusable memory. When the computer is turned off, RAM is erased.

ROM: Read-only memory, memory that cannot be changed.

Sequencer: A computer program or internal hardware device that records musical data for storage and possible manipulation.

Short-term memory (STM): Many psychologists recognize two types of memory storage in humans: short-term memory and long-term memory. STM is that memory that is limited in terms of storage (approximately 7 chunks of information) and is usually lost quickly.

Simulation software: A type of computer-assisted instruction program where students learn by performing activities in a context similar to a real world setting. Very often the real-life setting may be dangerous or impossible to reproduce in the real world. It is an experiential approach that allows students to learn by doing.

Software: The computer program.

TAP Master: A learning station centering on the development of rhythm developed by Temporal Acuity Products.

Tool software: A program that is designed to make some function easier to perform. This is sometimes referred to as application software.

Tutorial software: A type of computer-assisted instruction program that presents information on a specific topic.

Unattended speech effect: The effect of background speech (or other sounds) on the performance of some cognitive activity (e.g., reading).

Virtual reality (VR): A computer-created sensory environment that duplicates a real life experience.

Virus: A renegade computer program that is designed to sabotage a host computer in some fashion once it has been introduced into the system. It is usually placed on some storage media in a subversive manner and spreads into the host system in an unobtrusive manner.

Working memory: Short-term memory that comprises both storage and processing elements.